Sason VeSimcha

Sason

Compiled by
Mandell I. Ganchrow, M.D.

Edited by
Yisrael Epstein

Published by the

ששון ושמחה

VeSimcha

An Anthology of Divrei Torah for
Sheva Brachos

קול ששון וקול שמחה
קול חתן וקול כלה
קול מצהלות חתנים מחופתם . . .

❧

This volume is dedicated by

Martin Geller
מרדכי יעקב בן ישראל דוד

on the joyous occasion of his marriage to

Lauren Schor
עליזה בת חיים נחום

May 26, 1996   *8 Sivan 5756*

❧

*I am my beloved's
and my beloved is mine*

≈§ Table of Contents

Additional Divrei Torah

◆§ *Preface*

As soon as a Jewish child is born, it is blessed that it be raised toward a life of Torah, *chuppah* and good deeds. As the Rambam points out, the institution of marriage was initiated at the time of *mattan Torah*, for Torah is the cornerstone of Jewish family life and Jewish existence. In the modern world, the ultimate joy and *nachas* for parents, family and friends is to witness and participate in the wedding ceremony of a loved one.

Surely, the union of man and woman could not be accomplished without the intervention of the A-mighty. Rabbi Dr. Moshe Tendler explains the famous line in *Sanhedrin*, "The process of matchmaking is as difficult as the splitting of the Red Sea." Natural law dictates that water always flows. In formulating the natural law of water at the time of creation, however, G-d inserted a proviso, that at a given moment — seven days after the Jews' exodus from Egypt — the waters would part. At the moment Nachshon ben Aminadav jumped in, natural law was programmed so that the water would part and the Jewish people could travel over dry land through the Red Sea. Thereupon, the water returned to its usual nature, drowning the Egyptians who followed the Jews into the sea.

In this vein, natural law would dictate that human beings, with individual egos, backgrounds and family loyalties, not cleave to one another. Still, the Talmud declares, "Thirty days before a child is born, a heavenly voice calls out, 'the daughter of so-and-so [shall be betrothed] to so-and-so" — a reprogramming of natural law to be fulfilled at a later date.

It is with great happiness and pride that I am able to dedicate this volume to my wife of thirty-four years, Sheila, who has encouraged and supported me not only in my medical career but also in my work on behalf of *Klal Yisrael.* This book could not have become a reality without her. The idea for a volume on *sheva berachos* came from the frequency of requests from friends to say a *devar Torah* at a *sheva berachos seudah*.

I am extremely pleased that all of the profits from this book are being donated to a *kiruv* program of the Orthodox Union. As I begin my presidency of the Union, I am deeply cognizant not only of the great role it already plays in re-awakening the sparks of Judaism in our lost co-religionists but also of the increasing role it must play. As 1996 begins, the Orthodox Union has forty thousand young men and women in the N.C.S.Y. youth program, one thousand developmentally disabled children in the Yachad program, one thousand deaf children in Our Way, plus hundreds of youth in the Ukraine and in N.C.S.Y.'s Israel center.

I am indebted to Rabbi Pinchas Stolper, senior executive of the O.U., whose encouragement and assistance were invaluable. I owe a special thanks to Elly Edelman, whose technical assistance and input allowed this process to come to fruition. Rabbi Raphael Butler, our executive vice president, was there whenever needed to aid in making this book a success. Thanks also to Rabbi Bertram Leff for assisting in the final touches. This project could not have been accomplished without the input of Yisroel Epstein. Through Rabbi Butler, I found this young Torah scholar (who, incidentally, grew up one block from our home in Monsey). His talents as an editor and writer belie his young age and his efforts to bring uniformity and style to this *sefer* are greatly appreciated. The wonderful secretarial assistance of the staff of the Union was conducted by Malka Laks, with special assistance from Deborah Fishman, who allowed me to have all of the contributions placed into a meaningful order. Shelly Fliegelman, too, was instrumental in making this project successful.

I save my final note of appreciation for the dozens of contributors of *divrei* Torah without whom this effort could not have been made. We know that Torah is universal. The obligation to learn and to teach Torah is obligatory to all. I am extremely proud that the authors include a wide range of individuals: *rabbanim*, lawyers, academics, physicians and businessmen. This volume contains works that represent the transmission of Torah from generation to generation, as witnessed by the entries of Rabbi Nachum Muschel and his son, Dr. Michael Muschel, as well as the entries of myself, my sons, Ari and Elli, and my son-in-law, Dr. Paul Ratzker.

I hope the reader enjoys this volume and has many opportunities to share the *divrei* Torah. With so many contributions, one has the opportunity to learn much Torah as well as a *derech haTorah* from each chapter and to apply it appropriately.

Mandell I. Ganchrow, M.D.
June 1996 / Sivan 5756

Rabbi Dr. Moshe D. Tendler

Selected Halachos
of Sheva Berachos

1. For seven days following a wedding, the *sheva berachos* are said after *birkas hamazon*. If both the *chassan* and *kallah* were previously married, however, *sheva berachos* are said only the first day after the wedding.

2. *Sheva berachos* are said at every meal during those seven days (or, in the case of a second marriage, one day) at which ten men, including the *chassan*, are present. The ten must include a new guest — *panim chadashos* — who had not attended the wedding or any of the previous meals at which *sheva berachos* were said. On Shabbos and Yom Tov, *panim chadashos* are not required. The Midrash records the custom of arranging two meals each day so that the total number of *berachos* will be 98, counteracting the 98 curses that G-d threatens against the Jewish people (*Devarim* 28:15-68).

3. If ten men are not present (but three are) or if there is no *panim chadashos*, only the last two *berachos*, "*yotzeir ha'adam*" and "*hagafen*," are said, each over a separate cup of wine.

4. *Sheva berachos* are only said when the ten have eaten together. If, for example, the *chassan* and *kallah* ate dinner in a restaurant, they cannot invite other patrons to join them in *sheva berachos* at the

---

Rabbi Tendler is rav of Community Synagogue of Monsey, New York and Rosh Yeshiva of the Rabbi Isaac Elchanan Theological Seminary in New York City.

end of their meal (since they are not guests of the *chassan* but customers of the restaurateur), unless additional food is ordered for all in honor of the occasion.

5. A guest may not leave the meal before *sheva berachos* are said. If he knows in advance that he will need to depart early, he must make a mental note of this intention prior to washing his hands before the meal. Preferably, he should relay his intentions verbally to someone else. Or he may avoid the problem by not eating bread at all during the meal.

6. In order to permit as many guests as possible to be present for *sheva berachos*, the meal should not be unduly extended. Since it is probable that many guests will need to arise early the next morning for jobs or school, it would be wise to say *birkas hamazon* and *sheva berachos* immediately after the main course. Dessert, coffee, tea, dancing and celebrating can continue after the blessings for those whose schedules permit them to remain with the *chassan* and *kallah*.

7. The day of the wedding is considered the first day of the seven. If the wedding dinner extends past sundown, that evening and the next day are counted as day one. If the wedding dinner ends before sundown, day two begins that evening.

8. If the meal of the seventh day extends past sundown, *sheva berachos* are not said.

9. The preferred text for the special introductory poem, "*Devai Haseir*," said before *birkas hamazon*, is recorded in *Nachalas Shiva*:

דְּוַי הָסֵר וְגַם חָרוֹן. וְאָז אִלֵּם בְּשִׁיר יָרוֹן.
נְחֵנוּ בְּמַעְגְּלֵי צֶדֶק. שְׁעֵה בִרְכַּת בְּנֵי אַהֲרֹן.
שְׁעֵה בִרְכַּת יְשֻׁרוּן כְּבִרְכַּת בְּנֵי אַהֲרֹן.
בִּרְשׁוּת מָרָנָן וְרַבָּנָן וְרַבּוֹתַי נְבָרֵךְ אֱלֹהֵינוּ
שֶׁהַשִּׂמְחָה בִמְעוֹנוֹ שֶׁאָכַלְנוּ מִשֶּׁלּוֹ.

If the *mevareich* is a *kohein*, he amends the text to read:

שְׁעֵה בִרְכַּת בְּנֵי אַהֲרֹן.

10. According to Ashkenazic custom, the poem is not said on Shabbos and Yom Tov, because there is no expression of anguish (*devai*) on those days.

Sefer Bereishis

Rabbi Pinchas Stolper

פרשת בראשית
Parshas Bereishis

OF THE MANY BLESSINGS JEWS RECITE, the *sheva berachos* recited following the reading of the *kesubah* under the *chuppah* and during the following week are somewhat perplexing. The obvious question is: Over what are these blessings being recited? *"Hamotzi"* is recited over bread, *"hagafen"* over wine. But the first of the *sheva berachos* thanks G-d "Who created everything for His glory," a general philosophical statement that could be recited at almost any event. Why is it specifically reserved for the seven days of rejoicing following a wedding?

The second blessing, *"yotzeir ha'adam,"* thanks G-d for creating man. Wouldn't this blessing be more appropriately recited at a *bris milah* or following the *aliyah* a father receives when naming his newborn daughter? Why is it saved for an occasion when two mature people are being married?

This puzzle is solved when the blessing is examined carefully. The blessing uses the term *ha'adam*. If one refers back to the first time

---

Rabbi Stolper is senior executive of the Orthodox Union.

the word *ha'adam* is used in the Torah, one discovers that it is employed to describe the first human being, who was created, according to our Sages, male and female together.

Moreover, translated accurately, this blessing is not in the past tense (as it reads in most prayer books) but in the present tense. The blessing thanks G-d "Who creates *ha'adam*." In other words, this blessing is not over the creation of mankind in the past but over the creation of man in the present, and it is not about the creation of man *per se* but about the creation of *ha'adam*. "*Yotzeir ha'adam*" is a blessing over the event taking place before our eyes. At a wedding we are witness to the recreation of the original man/woman — *ha'adam*.

This also explains the significance of the first blessing, "*shehakol bara lichvodo*." Since the pinnacle and purpose of creation is the creation of man/woman, this blessing is recited at the reunion of man and woman into one, into *ha'adam*. The moment when man and woman stand under the *chuppah* together is when creation glows most brightly. It is the most appropriate time to glorify G-d for creation.

The third blessing follows this approach, thanking G-d "Who created" — past tense — "*ha'adam* in His image." The original *ha'adam*, man and woman together, was created *betzelem Elokim*, in the image of G-d. A man or woman living alone does not possess the full *tzelem Elokim*. Only through marriage, recreated as *ha'adam* under the marriage canopy before our very eyes, does the couple regain the *tzelem Elokim*. Acknowledging this, the blessing reverts back to the present tense, finishing with the words "*yotzeir ha'adam*," again thanking G-d "Who creates *ha'adam*."

The goal of marriage is to serve as the first step in the perfection of all humanity, and this notion is reflected in the fourth blessing: "The barren wife will rejoice and exalt when her children are gathered to her in joy." The barren wife refers to Zion, which remains barren until the Jewish people are gathered to her in joy with the arrival of the Messiah and the rebuilding of the Temple.

This blessing, too, concludes in the present tense, thanking G-d, "Who causes Zion to rejoice with her children." Each new Jewish home is another brick in the rebuilding of Zion and the Temple. Zion and her sons rejoice at each Jewish marriage because each one brings our nation one step closer to the final redemption. Every family carries within it the potential to be a driving force in the rejuvenation of the Jewish people.

The fifth blessing, describing the joy of the loving couple, asks, "May G-d make the beloved couple happy as He made happy His creation in Gan Eden." Happiness comes from attempting to reach the level of *ha'adam*, of Adam and Chavah before their sin, when mankind was at the pinnacle of perfection. This blessing identifies mankind's ability to learn from its past, from a time when the first man/woman were on the exemplary level that mankind is still capable of reaching. The present is our tool for achieving greatness in the future, but that can only happen when the present is patterned on the past.

The sixth and final blessing wraps up the package. We thank G-d for "creating joy and gladness, groom and bride, mirth, song, pleasure and delight, love and brotherhood and peace and companionship." In anticipation of the home the *chassan* and *kallah* will establish, permeated with Torah ideals, the blessing asks, "Speedily, O L-rd our G-d, may there be heard in the cities of Judah and the streets of Jerusalem the sound of joy and the sound of gladness, the sound of the groom and the sound of the bride." The blessing charges the bride and groom with their responsibility to become builders of Zion and the Temple, and includes a reminder that this task is the source of ultimate joy. "There is no sadness in the world for those who know the glaring light of truth," the *Chazon Ish* says. Ultimate joy results from binding one's life to purposefulness, to the rebuilding of Zion and the Temple.

My dear *chassan* and *kallah*, the seven days of festivity following a wedding mimic the seven days of creation. These seven days celebrate the creation of the marriage bond. Rav Yitzchak Hutner writes that under the *chuppah, chassan* and *kallah* receive a new soul and that "the essence of the joy of marriage derives from the fact that marriage is the source from which grows a new person." The joy of marriage is the rejoicing over the renewal of mankind — *ha'adam*. Your marriage will, we hope, forge a relationship that is spiritual, filled with creativity — a builder of eternity.

Rabbi Aaron Borow

פרשת בראשית
Parshas Bereishis

OUR SAGES SAY THAT ADAM AND CHAVAH were both beautiful and wise, and all of their basic needs were provided for in their earthly paradise. In the *berachah*, "*samei'ach tesamach*," we ask G-d to "make happy the beloved friends" the — *chassan* and *kallah* — "as You made happy Your creations in the Garden of Eden."

Does this blessing mean to say that we wish the *chassan* and *kallah* a life that is physically fulfilling? Are we asking that they be provided with good jobs and enjoy all the fruits of their labor?

Yes. But more than that. The great Biblical commentator, the *Or Hachaim*, explains that the first couple, after being placed in the Garden of Eden, were given the responsibility "*le'ovdah uleshomrah*, to work her and to guard her" (*Bereishis* 2:15). Did Adam and Chavah have to physically till the soil? Did they have to stand watch over the Garden? What is the meaning of this directive?

Rabbi Borow is rav of Congregation Nusach Hari-Bnai Zion in St. Louis, Missouri.

"*Le'ovdah* — these are the *mitzvos aseih*, the commands," our Sages say, "*uleshomrah* — these are the *mitzvos lo saaseih*, the prohibitions." The Garden of Eden was a spiritual world, the *Or Hachaim* explains. Adam was being told to pursue spirituality.

By extension, the Torah wants to express to all future generations that they are responsible not only for the physical elements of life but also for the spiritual ones. Just as a garden requires work — sowing, planting, cultivating, harvesting — and needs to be guarded from animals and men who might destroy its fruits, so too, human beings need the proper spiritual attention. Only by working to advance one's spirituality and by guarding against the deleterious effects of a morally questionable society can man insure his well-being.

What can one do, specifically, to further a commitment to the Torah's way of life? One example comes from *Parshas Shoftim*. "Appoint for yourselves judges and officers in all your gates," the Torah commands (*Devarim* 16:18). The *Shelah* extends this command to each individual. A Jew, he writes, must judge and guard his own personal gates — one's eyes, ears and mouth must be protected from seeing, hearing, tasting what is unclean.

One must also judge carefully before speaking, especially a *chassan* and *kallah*. Every word should be expressed in a loving and caring way. Just as a kind word will build a strong relationship, a harsh word can injure it.

My dear *chassan* and *kallah*, use your eyes to see all the good things of your beloved friend. Hear all the wonderful praises being spoken about each other. Taste the delicious food prepared in your honor. Take care to insure that all the marvelous things entering your gates these past few days remain that way. Judge carefully what you see and hear; don't jump to conclusions and always give the benefit of the doubt. You have made a fine beginning together cultivating your garden. May you continue on the path of Torah and *mitzvos*, build a house of faith, and give great joy to your families and friends and all of *Klal Yisrael*.

Rabbi Nachum Muschel

פרשת נח
Parshas Noach

SHEVA BRACHOS CELEBRATES THE SUPREME MOMENT in the lives of a new couple — their *kiddushin*, an act of consecration, sealing their troth and love for each other. With this blessed union the two commence the fulfillment of their hopes and dreams of building a home of their own to serve as a tower of Jewish strength, human dignity and personal beauty.

In *Parshas Noach*, the Torah records the story of the tower of Bavel that the people of the post-flood generation built to achieve harmony and security. G-d Himself attested to the ability of the generation to attain their goal. They were an intelligent and an industrious society, capable of seeing the fulfillment of their ambition. Yet, for all their potential, they failed to complete the project. They had to be dismantled, lowered, humbled. What were they lacking?

A careful reading of the text indicates the cause of their undoing. The Torah, with a seemingly innocuous statement, describes how the people

Rabbi Muschel is dean emeritus of the Adolph Schreiber Hebrew Academy of Rockland and rav of Congregation Hadar in Monsey, New York.

frustrated their own plans: "And it was when they travelled from the east (*kedem*), they found a valley in the land of Shinar and they dwelt there" (*Bereishis* 11:2). *Kedem* connotes more than the direction one finds on a compass; it suggests the Divine Presence of G-d. The Garden of Eden was planted near *kedem*, as noted in the fifth blessing of the *sheva berachos*. By travelling away from *kedem*, away from the center of G-dly influence, the generation demonstrated that it wanted a society free from G-d's authority. Indeed, the Midrash renders this *pasuk*, "They removed themselves from *Kadmon*" — from the Earliest One, from G-d.

What was the result? "They found a valley in the land of Shinar and they dwelt there." As a consequence of their misguided journey, they arrived at a valley, a low point in human history.

The danger of abandoning a spiritual existence is repeated in the story of Lot, Avraham's nephew, who left his uncle's household and relocated to the evil city of Sodom. As the *pasuk* describes it: "Lot travelled from *kedem*" (13:11). His move away from Avraham was a move away from holiness. As a result, Lot was promptly scathed by the destruction of Sodom, which took his wife, his home and his fortune.

With the punishment for such behavior being swift and harsh, one wonders how the builders of the tower achieved any success at all. How were they able to prosper long enough to see their tower reach a height that, according to the Midrash, took a lifetime to climb? Once again, the subtleties of the text prove enlightening.

The Torah informs us that "the whole land was one language and a common resolve" (11:1). Because they were united, they were successful. No matter how evil their plans were, they were able to carry them out because they stood together. Their success demonstrates the high regard G-d has for human solidarity. Consequently, in order to frustrate their effort, G-d had to disrupt that unity. Then the people self-destructed.

The Talmud relates that the purpose of the tower was threefold: to serve as a haven in case of another flood, as a temple in which to worship idols, and as a gateway to the heavens through which war could be declared on G-d (*Sanhedrin* 109b). "And the L-rd descended to see the city and the tower the people had built" (11:5). While the people continued to build their tower, G-d decided to pay them a visit and inspect their behavior. G-d did not prejudge them, notes Rav Samson

Raphael Hirsch, but instead descended to examine their motivation. What was objectionable was not the physical construction of the tower, but the intent behind its construction. "We will make for ourselves a name" (11:4), they declared. Rather than glorifying G-d's Name, they sought to make a name for themselves. Rather than applying their new advances in technical prowess to pursuits that would bring them closer to G-d, they used their technology to rebel against Him.

In response, G-d frustrated their efforts. He multiplied their languages and scattered them, sending them into confusion, destroying the very unity that had alllowed them to prosper. They suffered because they remained oblivious to the fact that "if G-d is not involved in the building of a structure, to naught are all the efforts of its builders" (*Tehillim* 127:1).

My dear *chassan* and *kallah,* both of you are uniquely blessed, possessing a common language, a common resolve, and a mutual love for each other. You have intelligence and the academic training of your careers. You share a rich Jewish education enhanced by families that serve as models for what a Jewish home should be. You are united in your ambition to build a Torah home and raise a Torah family. You have the understanding and the determination to adorn your home, your tower, with G-dly blessings and with the beauty of our traditions. May you go on this journey with G-d and His blessings, with your talents, resolve and newly acquired unity, and build your own indestructible tower, which will proclaim the glory of G-d until the end of days.

Rabbi Nachman Kahana

פרשת לך לך
Parshas Lech Lecha

THE TORAH'S PLACEMENT OF CONSECUTIVE *PESUKIM* is never incidental. The Talmud is filled with examples of the Sages being *darish semuchin*, asking, "Why was this passage placed next to that passage?" then establishing a connection between the seemingly unrelated pair. Sometimes these connections have important halachic ramifications; other times they come to offer practical advice. But always they underscore the precision of the Torah's written text.

Even when the two *pesukim* are found in two separate *parshios* we search for a common denominator. The last *pasuk* in *Parshas Noach*, "Terach died in Charan" (*Bereishis* 11:32), followed by the first *pasuk* in *Parshas Lech Lecha*, "And the L-rd said to Avram, Go for yourself from your land, from your birthplace and from your father's house to the land that I will show you" (12:1), seem to tell a straightforward story: Avram's journey away from Charan. But as the Midrash notes, these two *pesukim* cannot be in chronological order.

Rabbi Kahana is rav of the Young Israel of the Old City in Jerusalem.

Terach, the Torah informed us a few *pesukim* earlier (11:26), was 70 years old when his son Avram was born, and Avram was 75 when he departed for the Holy Land (12:4). This means Terach was 145 when his son left home — and he lived for another 60 years, to the age of 205, according to the *pasuk* (11:32). Obviously, this means that the order of the *pesukim* was switched. Why? What accounts for this reverse timetable?

The Midrash clarifies the Torah's intent with a dialogue that took place between Avram and G-d. When Avram was told by G-d to leave his father, he was hesitant. "I will leave," he said, "and because of me they will debase the Name of Heaven and say, 'He abandoned his father in his old age and went off.' " Avram, who was viewed as G-d's quintessential servant, argued that he would appear to be violating one of G-d's basic codes of human behavior. G-d responded by releasing Avram from the obligation to honor one's parents, and alleviated his fear by recording in the Torah these events in reverse order: Terach's death before Avram's departure (*Bereishis Rabbah* 39:7).

G-d's command and Avram's acquiescence serve as a model for all generations. From the moment of birth, a person is an inseparable part of the family unit. Even when away from home, the firm bonds of family hold a person securely to his beloved parents and siblings. Nevertheless, a profound psychological change comes when one is brought to the *chuppah* by those same beloved and devoted parents who were the center of one's life until that moment. The *chuppah* declares that the young couple standing underneath is now independent. Although their lives have been saliently shaped by past experiences and have been, to a large extent, in the hands of others, from this moment on they take charge of their lives and make their decisions independently.

There are rewards for this independence. The Talmud declares, "A change of place tears up any evil decree against a person, as it is written, 'And the L-rd said to Avram, Go for yourself from your land, from your birthplace . . .' followed by, 'And I will make you into a great nation" ' (*Rosh Hashanah* 16b). In following G-d's directive and moving on, Avram and Sarai were rewarded with the child they thought they would never have. Through that child they were guaranteed a great future, all for embarking on their Divine mission. Their move was more than just a physical change of place. It was a spiritual ascent, transferring them to the Holy Land, to holiness itself. It amounted to a promotion of their station in life.

But that move did not come free from pain. Avram and Sarai had to undergo the travails of famine and war, thus fulfilling the words of our Sages that "Eretz Yisrael is acquired through hardship." Such is the quest for sanctity: The level of difficulty is commensurate with the rewards of choosing such a path. And the first step is *lech lecha*.

Standing under the *chuppah* with the recognition of this newly found independence and its concomitant responsibilities is one of the most dramatic moments a young couple experiences. It, too, carries the weight of certain hardships — the natural difficulties of moving on. This is the dilemma Avram had to contend with and it continues to the present day. But G-d informs us that, as difficult as it may be on a human level, the time comes when people must face their personal destiny and establish themselves as a new family within their nation.

My dear *chassan* and *kallah,* every generation has responsibilities that are paramount to its time and cannot suffer delay. The prime call to conscientious Jews today — as it was to Avram and Sarai in their time — is to rebuild Eretz Yisrael. As a new family unit within the community of the Jewish people, you balance your conscience against your family ties. The ultimate satisfaction to your families, however, comes from this very commitment, from your efforts to fulfill the destiny of the Jewish people, from your fulfillment of the *mitzvah* of *lech lecha.*

Rabbi Menachem Genack

פרשת וירא
Parshas Vayeira

I MMEDIATELY AFTER THE TORAH PORTRAYS the dramatic events of the *Akeidah*, it records that Avraham was informed that his sister-in-law, Milka, had given birth to several children, among them, Besuel, who in turn fathered Rivkah. By placing Rivkah's genealogy next to the story of the *Akeidah*, the Torah makes it clear that her lineage is an integral part of the *Akeidah*. A common phrase testifies to this connection. The *Akeidah* is introduced with the words, "And it was after these events that G-d tested Avraham" (*Bereishis* 22:1). Similarly, news of Rivkah's birth begins, "And it was after these events that it was told to Avraham" about his family (22:20). In fact, when the *Akeidah* is read on Rosh Hashanah, the *pesukim* detailing Rivkah's birth are also read. Apparently the two are linked. But what is their relationship to each other?

Rav Joseph B. Soloveitchik suggests that news of Rivkah's birth was part of the *Akeidah* itself, an extra dimension to the most challenging of

Rabbi Genack, rabbinic administrator of the Orthodox Union's kashrus division, is rav of Congregation Shomrei Emunah in Englewood, New Jersey.

Avraham's tests. There stood Avraham Avinu, ever loyal to *Hakadosh Baruch Hu,* faithful, never questioning. For all his heroic deeds, G-d grants him, in his very old age, a son. He is then commanded to sacrifice that son. At the same time, Avraham looks around and sees those who are much less worthy, who sacrificed little or not at all, having children, one after another, without pain, without torment, naturally. Still, Avraham never questions G-d's will.

After the *Akeidah*, Rashi notes, G-d informs Avraham that Yitzchak's mate has been born. According to Rashi, "it was told to Avraham" means that it was told prophetically — from G-d Himself. The spiritual ecstasy of the *Akeidah* did not dissipate easily. Avraham's fiery commitment, his devotion to G-d, as proved by the *Akeidah*, needed to be perpetuated. The *Akeidah* would have to continue through Yitzchak, who would marry Rivkah and propagate the legacy of Avraham. Though the *Akeidah* was a unique event in human history, the commitment it demonstrated was not isolated; it was transmitted through Yitzchak to future generations, to the people who stood at Sinai, to the nation that continues a day-to-day schedule of Torah study and *mitzvah* observance.

The challenge of the *Akeidah*, of sacrifice on the part of the Jewish people for their Father in Heaven, continues to our present day. With Rivkah's birth and subsequent marriage to Yitzchak, the test of the *Akeidah* was forever embedded in Jewish life and Jewish history. Rivkah, as much as Yitzchak, was part of the story of the *Akeidah*.

Another lesson is learned from the *Akeidah*. Avraham set out with Yitzchak toward Har Hamoriah and "on the third day, Avraham lifted his eyes and saw the place from afar" (22:4). Why was the *Akeidah*'s location kept from Avraham for three days? Rashi explains that had G-d revealed it to him immediately, the claim would be that Avraham reacted hastily; momentarily stunned and confused, he consented. Had he had time to think over what he was about to do, he would have reconsidered. Never would he have consented.

These three days of preparation correspond to another three days, says the Midrash. "And it was on the third day" — following three days of preparation — that the revelation at Sinai took place (*Shemos* 19:16). The connection is enlightening. Often people reach a certain state of religious fervor that, though genuine, does not last. Over a period of time their passion evaporates. When Avraham consented to sacrifice his son on the very day he received G-d's command to do so, he displayed a level of commitment that was intense, but not necessarily deep, not quite durable. Avraham showed the depth of his commitment when he acquiesced on the third day. Given time for deliberation, for sobering, his passion still burned. Time is the test of the great religious personality.

The Jewish people's acceptance of the Torah also demonstrates this attribute, a long-term commitment, a passion for Divine service that continually burns, that does not grow faint with the passage of time. The great responsibility of keeping the Torah requires this commitment, this passion. It is what has enabled the Jewish people to survive through both the calamitous times and the golden ages. Whether facing fierce persecution or comfortable apathy, the Jewish nation has proved itself to be steadfast. It has passed the test of time.

My dear *chassan* and *kallah,* the instrument for the transmission of our glorious traditions, for the perpetuation of our historic mission, is the Jewish family. The Torah makes that much clear with the introduction of Rivkah after the *Akeidah*. No experience, no matter how exalted, can be communicated and sustained through time outside the context of family. Your friends and relatives gather to celebrate with you the *shivas yemei hamishteh* and recitation of the *sheva brachos* not just as a personal occasion, but also for what it signifies — the essential link in the chain of our *mesorah* and the conduit for our divinely endowed mission.

Rabbi Dr. Daniel H. Mehlman

פרשת חי' שרה

Parshas Chayei Sarah

LOOKING UPON YOUR GLOWING FACES this day, one reaffirms that nothing in life happens by chance. Everything has the imprint of *hashgachah peratis*, divine guidance, and this is especially true in the selection of one's lifelong mate. G-d surely directed your two lives to meet and unite in marriage.

"*Ezri mei'im Hashem*, My help comes from G-d," wrote David Hamelech in *Tehillim* (121:2). The same word, *eizer*, help, is used by the Torah to define a wife and we echo our king's words by saying that this *eizer* is certainly *mei'im Hashem*.

In *Parshas Chayei Sarah*, the Torah reports the story of Yitzchak and Rivkah, who represent a most magnificent picture of G-d's plan for the ultimate relationship between husband and wife. As Avraham's servant, Eliezer, was returning from Nachor with Rivkah, "Yitzchak went to pray in the field" (*Bereishis* 24:63). What did he pray for? For a special woman of *chessed* and *emes* to enter his life, say our Sages. Rivkah was that person.

Rabbi Mehlman is rav of the Lido Beach Synagogue in Lido Beach, New York.

The Torah goes on to describe Rivkah as a beautiful person, beautiful from within and beautiful from without, a person who possessed special character, "and she was to him for a wife, and he loved her" (24:67). Love was a most important ingredient in their relationship.

Once, says the Midrash, there was a man who was traveling through the desert. It was hot. He was hungry, thirsty and tired. He came upon a palm tree that bore sweet dates and cast a comforting shade, sheltering a spring of cool water. He feasted upon the dates, drank his fill of the water and sat down to rest in the shade.

When the time came for him to depart, he turned thankfully to the tree and said, "My dear date palm, how shall I bless you? If I wish you sweet fruit — it is already sweet. If I hope you cast fine shadows — they are so now. And if it is a cool spring I wish — you have it. So I bless you thus: May every sapling that grows from your seed be just like you.

My dear chassan and kallah, you, too, are fully blessed. Each of you prayed for a worthy and noble spouse, and both of you were rewarded with one — one who is beautiful from within and from without. Love evinces sharing, concern, reaching out. I see this profound love between you, easily observing how you extend to each other love, compassion, and understanding. It seems like an all-encompassing love, a celestial love, full of genuineness. As you go forward on your journey of life together, you are joined with our hopes and prayers that the special relationship you experience at this most exhilarating moment continue throughout your lifetime.

Rabbi Milton H. Polin

פרשת חי׳ שרה
Parshas Chayei Sarah

MY DEAR *CHASSAN* AND *KALLAH,* this moment, as you unite your two separate lives into one and sanctify your marriage, is simultaneously an end and a beginning. It is the end of your courtship and engagement; it is simultaneously the beginning of your courtship and marriage. How long it may have taken from the time you first met until you decided to marry and announced your engagement is really immaterial. Perhaps it was love at first sight. I pray that the beginning of your courtship and marriage will be love at first sight. I trust that the inner joy that expresses itself on your faces is an indication that it is indeed love at first sight.

The Torah, in fact, advocates love at first sight! That might come as a surprise to theatergoers who sing with the "Fiddler on the Roof" cast, "Matchmaker, matchmaker, make me a match." Yet, the Torah does report and advocate love at first sight!

Rabbi Polin is rav of the Kingsway Jewish Center in Brooklyn, New York.

Ah, but what kind of love at first sight? The most detailed love story in the entire Torah is that of Yitzchak and Rivkah. Briefly, Avraham Avinu sent his trusted Eliezer to bring a wife for Yitzchak. Eliezer, following Avraham's orders, goes back to his master's family's homeland and prays to G-d at the city well: "Let the maiden to whom I say, 'Please, lower your jar that I may drink,' and who replies, 'Drink, and I will also water your camels — let her be the one whom You have decreed for Your servant, Yitzchak" (*Bereishis* 24:13). As soon as Eliezer finished that prayer, Rivkah came to the well and did exactly as Eliezer had asked for. Eliezer came to Rivkah's home and related his experience, his prayer and Rivkah's deed.

The story is told in such great detail that the Midrash comments, "The conversation of the Patriarchs' servants is more beautiful before G-d than the Torah of their descendants, for the story of Eliezer is repeated by the Torah, whereas many of the Torah's principles are given only thorough allusion" (*Bereishis Rabbah* 60:8).

Why so much attention to the story? Because Eliezer immediately fell in love with Rivkah's act of kindness, her expression of *chessed*.

So Rivkah followed Eliezer back to Canaan and caught her first glimpse of Yitzchak. "And Yitzchak went out to meditate in the field toward evening" (24:63). Rashi cites the Midrash, "By meditation, prayer is meant." Rivkah's first glimpse of Yitzchak was of him at prayer. She fell in love with his act of piety, his *tefillah*.

That's what the Torah means by love at first sight. If the first thing one notices about the *kallah* is her *chessed*, if the first thing one notices about the *chassan* is his *tefillah* — and Torah and *middos* — then there is a couple who embody Torah-true love at first sight.

The look in your eyes, both of you, is the look of love at first sight. You, *chassan,* see in your *kallah* her wonderful acts of *chessed*. You, *kallah,* see in your *chassan* his devotion to *Hakadosh Baruch Hu,* his *tefillah*, and Torah and *middos*. With this kind of love at first sight may Hashem grant you blessings and happiness as you establish a *bayit ne'eman beYisrael*.

David M. Srulowitz

פרשת תולדות
Parshas Toldos

THE QUINTESSENTIAL FAMILY EXPERIENCE is found in a *sheva berachos* celebration. Unlike the wedding, which is filled with formalities, guests and anxiety, *sheva berachos* is more intimate and more relaxed; the pace is slower, less hectic. There is time for longer conversations and deeper contemplation. That, in turn, allows one to reflect upon the concept of family, the development of family, and the welcoming of a new family into the House of Israel.

For these reflections, *Parshas Toldos* is opportune; it is the ultimate Biblical family drama. Every word in the *parshah* concerns family and no other *parshah* in the Torah contains so many details about so many relationships: a husband and wife praying for a child; brothers exchanging a birthright; G-d promising His follower a dynasty; a king discovering "brother and sister" to be, in fact, husband and wife; a son unsealing his father's wells; parents-in-law disappointed by their daughter-in-law; a father blessing his sons; a brother plotting to kill his brother; a mother instructing her son to flee to his grandfather.

David Srulowitz is a writer living in New York City.

That's the *parshah* on fast-forward. Spouses, children, siblings, in-laws, parents, grandparents — all playing out their roles and relationships. An examination of these roles and the people who played them is, especially at this time and place, instructive.

The *parshah's* title, *Toldos*, can be translated as Generations, and, as the *parshah* demonstrates throughout, the durability of generations is sustained by faith and adherence to Torah values.

The *parshah* begins, "These are the generations of Yitzchak, son of Avraham; Avraham bore Yitzchak" (*Bereishis* 25:19). The seeming redundancy is actually a veiled message from the *pasuk,* comments the Ramban; Yitzchak had the exclusive privilege of continuing his father's dynasty. Only Yitzchak — and not his half brother, Yishmael — is to be considered the progeny of Avraham, the *pasuk* is saying.

Yet, one of the last *pesukim* in the previous *parshah, Chayei Sarah,* states: "These are the generations of Yishmael, son of Avraham, who Hagar the Egyptian bore" (25:12). Yishmael, too, it seems, could trace his lineage to Avraham Avinu and he has the verse to prove it.

But even a quick review of the two *pesukim* reveals a contrast. Both are referred to as sons of Avraham, but while Avraham is also given credit for bearing Yitzchak, Hagar, Yismael's mother, is credited for the birth of their son. The *Keli Yakar*, therefore, offers a nature-nurture explanation for the Torah's divergent descriptions of the two brothers.

The term son — *ben* — is nurture related, he writes; it can be applied even to relationships where there is no blood connection. One's students, say Chazal, are considered his *banim* (*Sifri*, *Devarim* 6:7). But the Hebrew term *yalad*, to bear, is nature related; it refers specifically to one's natural birth.

Yishmael, though he was the son of Avraham, is considered to have been born only to his mother, Hagar, for he adopted her nature. His relationship to his father was only one of a *ben*, limited to that which he learned from Avraham. But his education by Avraham was squelched by his natural character as he set out on a life of evil. It was only Yitzchak who had both his father's nature and his nurture.

The transfer of character from parent to child, whether by nature or nurture, is evident again just a few *pesukim* later. Yitzchak and Rivkah, who are barren, pray for a child and, as the *pasuk* phrases it, "G-d was persuaded by him, and his wife, Rivkah, became pregnant" (35:21). Why was G-d swayed by him and not by her? Because, the Talmud informs, "the prayer of the righteous who is a child of the righteous does not compare to the prayer of the righteous who is a child of the evil" (*Yevamos* 64a).

Rivkah, who did not come from righteous stock, became righteous on her own and suffers the setback of having a less than worthy father. The *pasuk* describes her as "Rivkah, the daughter of Besuel. . .the sister of Lavan" (25:20), in order to praise her for not following their example, says Rashi. Though she came from this family, she went on to become Rivkah, Matriarch of the Jewish nation.

Nevertheless, the *Keli Yakar* points out, her heritage comes back to haunt her. Our Sages teach that children follow in the footsteps of their mother's brothers. Hence, Rivkah has a son, Eisav.

Her other son, Yaakov, with Rivkah and Yitzchak's blessing, goes to his uncle Lavan's house and eventually marries his two daughters, Rachel and Leah. They, like their aunt, do not pick up their father's evil ways. They, too, become Matriarchs.

The overwhelming lesson of this *parshah* is that children, on the one hand, have the ability to break away from their upbringing and move on to build their own, independent persona, and on the other hand, always remain attached to their parents and affected by their parents' behavior.

Along these lines, the Gemara (*Sanhedrin* 27b) brings an apparent contradiction: In one *pasuk* it says, "Children will not die for [the sins of] their fathers" (*Devarim* 24:16), and, in another *pasuk* it says, "He redeems the sins of fathers upon children, grandchildren, third generation and fourth generation" (*Shemos* 34:7). What accounts for this discrepancy?

The difference, explains the Gemara, lies in the behavior of the children. Those who follow the ways of their parents are held accountable not only for their own sins but for their ancestors' sins as well. But those who break away from the pattern of their parents' evil behavior are clean from past iniquities.

My dear *chassan* and *kallah,* how fortunate it is to offer blessings to a couple such as yourselves, rooted in Torah not just by personal choice but also by family tradition. Your upbringing, your education, your lineage, earn you the title of "*tzaddik ben tzaddik*," the righteous children of righteous parents, and give you the *zechus avos* that will no doubt benefit you in times of need. We are confident that you will succeed in passing on these qualities to the next generation, and, in doing so, renew the words Yitzchak spoke to his son, Yaakov, centuries ago, "G-d shall give you the blessings of Avraham, to you and to your children with you" (28:4).

Rabbi Moshe Morduchowitz

פרשת תולדות
Parshas Toldos

THE TORAH DOES NOT REVEAL how Avraham and Sarah met, but does give some insight into how they interrelated. After a famine struck the land of Canaan, Avraham tells Sarah, "Behold, I know that you are a beautiful woman. And when the Egyptians see you they will say, 'This is his wife,' and they will kill me and keep you alive. Please say you are my sister so that I will benefit for your sake and my soul will live because of you" (*Bereishis* 12:11-13).

They talk. Avraham communicates his fears to Sarah and a *modus operandi* is formulated.

Avraham and Sarah's son, Yitzchak, is confronted with an identical situation when a famine again strikes the Holy Land, and he travels to Gerar. "And the people of the place inquired after his wife and he said, 'She is my sister'; for he was afraid to say 'my wife' — lest the men of the place kill me for Rivkah, as she is beautiful" (26:7).

In contrast to Avraham's story, the Torah does not record any

Rabbi Moshe Morduchowitz is dean of the Yeshiva of the West Side and rav of the West Side Institutional Synagogue, both in New York City.

conversation between them, any discussion of how they planned to deal with the danger they were to face prior to entering the land. In fact, the Torah records very little dialogue between them at all.

Another difference between the two stories is how the true relationship of husband and wife is discovered. In Avraham's case, an angel appears to Pharaoh and threatens him, but in Yitzchak's case, Avimelech, king of Gerar, himself discovers the truth when he sees Yitzchak and Rivkah being intimate with each other.

Moreover, the Torah records that Yitzchak loved his wife (24:67), a fact not explicitly mentioned of Avraham and Sarah. From a reading of the text, it seems fair to posit that the Torah is delineating two typologies of successful marriages; one where communication is explicit, the other where it is implicit.

By revealing these aspects of the interrelations of our Patriarchs and Matriarchs, the Torah teaches that, by marrying, a couple does not embark on something novel or new. Their fathers and mothers did it before them. Two people from two different backgrounds and two distinct parentages can become soulmates. Two bodies, say the scholars of kabbalah, can become one soul. However, work, commitment and stick-to-itness are required. Anything meaningful in life requires effort.

The Rambam, in codifying the laws of marriage in his *Mishnah Torah*, incorporates the words of the Talmud, waxing eloquent and decidedly non-halachic. He writes: "Our Sages commanded that a man honor his wife more than himself and love her more than seems necessary . . . following the longing of his heart and removing everything he hates" (*Hilchos Ishus* 15:19-20).

My dear *chassan* and *kallah,* the Rambam isolates a vital element for a successful relationship of love. One should not react defensively, saying, "I didn't know you didn't like this person or that you didn't like that food." Anticipating one's mate's wishes is the crucial element for a successful marriage. "In such a manner," concludes the Rambam, "their life together will be pleasant and praiseworthy."

Rabbi Steven Pruzansky

פרשת ויצא
Parshas Vayeitzei

T HE COURTSHIP OF YAAKOV AND RACHEL, detailed in *Parshas Vayeitzei*, was unusual by our standards. Yaakov met Rachel at a public well and in a matter of moments determined that she was destined to be his wife. He entered the house of his future father-in-law, Lavan, and agreed to work for him for seven years to win the hand of Rachel.

And the rest is Jewish history: Lavan's deception; Yaakov's marriage first to Leah, then to Rachel; the birth of their children. Yet many of the *pesukim* describing these events seem odd.

After Lavan unenthusiastically agreed to their marriage, "Yaakov worked for Rachel seven years, but they were in his eyes like a few days, in his love for her" (*Bereishis* 29:20). Typically, the opposite is true: When two people are in love, even a short separation seems to them an unbearable eternity. How is one to understand Yaakov's emotions?

More puzzling is Yaakov's behavior when the seven years end. He brusquely confronts his father-in-law. "Bring me my wife," he demands,

---

Rabbi Pruzansky is rav of Congregation Bnai Yeshurun in Teaneck, New Jersey.

"and I will live with her" (29:21). Rashi comments that even the most unsophisticated boor would not speak so crudely. How is one to understand Yaakov's words?

Yaakov is then tricked by Lavan, who switches Rachel for Leah and then demands that he work another seven years before allowing him to marry Rachel. Seven years and one week have passed from the time he met her at the well and at last she becomes his wife. But they do not have children; Yaakov's only children are born to Leah. After her fourth son, "Rachel saw that she had bore Yaakov no children; and Rachel became jealous of her sister and said to Yaakov, 'Give me children; if not, I am dead.' And Yaakov was furious at Rachel and said, 'Am I in place of G-d Who withheld from you fruits of the womb?' " Rachel responds by giving Yaakov her maid, Bilhah, to bear him children, "and I too will be built up from her" (30:1-3).

More questions. Why did Yaakov react so angrily? Was he oblivious to his wife's despondence? Why did Rachel equate her childlessness with death? Why does she respond by offering her maid to her husband? How would she benefit from children that Bilhah would produce?

To understand the story one must read the text keeping the underlying current that flows through the *parshah* in mind. That explains all the difficulties. Yaakov and his wives knew they were not just raising a family; they were establishing the house of Israel. They were chosen to build a dynasty started by Avraham and Sarah, and continued by Yitzchak and Rivkah. To the Patriarchs and Matriarchs, marriage was not an act of romance and children were not simply the results of reproduction. Their concept of family, and all their subsequent behavior, focused on the burning desire to implement G-d's will and produce the tribes of G-d, upon which His nation would be built. Consequently, marriage and family life were driven by the extraordinary circumstances in which they lived, in accordance with their unique status as the founders of the nation of G-d.

Yaakov's seven-year wait was not characterized by uncontrollable physical longings. His sole desire to found a nation required him to marry a worthy ancestress and upon recognizing Rachel as such a person, he was on his way to that goal. If G-d meant for him to wait, he would do so patiently. The seven years passed quickly.

But once the delay was over, he was anxious to proceed to the next stage — having children — as soon as possible. Yaakov's impatient demand to Lavan reflected his zeal to carry out his Divine mission. After all the conditions he had agreed upon were met, G-d's plan for the Jewish people required immediate execution.

Rachel and Leah shared their husband's prescience and were completely focused on their Divine missions as well. But while Leah was able to achieve success, Rachel was not. Rachel, the Midrash explains, was jealous of her sister's righteousness (*Bereishis Rabbah* 71:6). She feared her sister was more worthy than she was and therefore was blessed with all of Yaakov's children. Without children of her own, Rachel was dead — she would play no role in the formation of the Jewish nation. So Rachel pursued another route. Through Bilhah, she would be able to have a share in raising — if not giving birth to — the tribes of G-d.

As for Yaakov, the *Or Hachaim* explains, he was not angry at Rachel but angry over her statement, "I am dead," because all the words of the righteous, even when qualified, have a strong impact in the heavens. Yaakov was upset that Rachel cursed herself. He was also disturbed that she demanded of him, "Give me," rather than asking, "Pray for me."

Our ancestors shared a perspective on marriage completely different from that which most people have today. This perspective deserves our attention and understanding. Marriage is more than the union of two people; it is an act of national significance, an event with historic repercussions. The *sheva brachos* are said in the presence of ten, signifying that the Jewish family must find its rightful place in the national community and not exist solely as a personal institution. Marriage completes the human being and is a prerequisite for the assumption of a more active role in serving G-d and the Jewish people.

My dear *chassan* and *kallah,* you have provided the Jewish people with another building block, contributing to the fulfillment of G-d's will for Israel. By perceiving your marriage in this light and committing yourselves, your energies and your talents to the strengthening of our Torah, our nation and our homeland, you help further the Jewish mission and secure the Jewish future.

Rabbi Yosef B. Wolicki

פרשת וישלח
Parshas Vayishlach

J EWISH TRADITION COMPARES THE WEDDING DAY to Yom Kippur for the bride and groom. For the two of them, the day is like a personal Yom Kippur, on which they engage in *cheshbon hanefesh*. On that day of transition from being single to being married, they introspect and reflect on their past and their plans for the future.

In *Parshas Vayishlach*, Yaakov also finds himself at a critical turning point in his life. He is about to meet his brother Eisav after a prolonged separation. He prepares himself for this challenge by composing some questions and answers. These questions and answers help him to define who he is and what is important to him; what his values are and what are his priorities.

Yaakov's questions and answers contain an important message for all of us and especially for the *chassan* and *kallah*.

The first question is, "To whom do you belong?" (*Bereishis* 32:18). How do you relate to the past? What are your roots? Is the past important in your life? Is it something on which you hope to build, or

---

Rabbi Wolicki is rav of the New Synagogue in Netanya, Israel.

will you cast it aside? Do you identify with your forebears, or do you feel detached from them?

The second question is, "Where are you going?" What is your vision of the future? What are your goals and aspirations? What kind of home will you build? What values will you inculcate into your children? What are your hopes and dreams?

Finally, "Whose is all this that is before you?" All the gifts that you have, your talents, your strengths. What do you intend to do with them? What will you share? What will you keep to yourself?

For Yaakov, there are only two answers for the three questions. For us, it must be the same.

To whom do you belong and where are you going? Yaakov answered with one answer, "Your servant, Yaakov." There is no division between the past and the future. They are inextricably linked. We are all continuations of the past. We build upon it, and extend the drama of Jewish history and the purity of the Jewish people into the future. The couple before us become a new link in the chain that connects our past with our future.

Yaakov answers the third question, "Whose is all this?," with the words, "It is a gift, freely given" (32:19). We must all answer the same way. We must be ready to give of ourselves, freely, to assure the future. You must be prepared to dedicate all your talents and love to build the home of which you dream, and to raise children in whom you can take pride.

My dear *chassan* and *kallah,* the chuppah under which you now stand is symbolic of that future home that you begin to build. The design of the *chuppah* has an important message of its own. It has a roof, but no walls. Instead of walls, which insulate and exclude, there are people who have played significant roles in your lives — people who nurtured you, who educated you, who gave their love freely, and who continue to love you with all their hearts.

They are your past and the foundation of your future. They gave freely of their gifts with all their hearts to help you grow and reach this day. And as they gave to you, so we pray that you will give to others, inspiring them with the beauty of the Jewish home. May your home be a source of joy to you, a source of *nachas* to your parents, and a source of new strength for the people of Israel.

Rabbi Yehoshua Balkany

פרשת וישב
Parshas Vayeishev

UR SAGES ENUMERATE SEVEN LEVELS of heaven. A marriage is celebrated with the recitation of seven blessings, a joyous expression of thanksgiving for the union ordained in those very heavens. As these blessings are pronounced, all wish that the newlyweds' dreams, aspirations and prayers reach the highest heavens. All hope that the couple will build a home of heaven on earth.

What an ideal this is! Everyone knows that life has its burdens and boundaries, its difficulties and drawbacks. Can the ideal possibly be fulfilled — or is it a simple, idle thought, a foolish dream?

In order to appreciate the validity of these and all dreams, and to understand the relation of dreams to reality, one may consult *Parshas Vayeishev*. In that *parshah*, Yosef dreams that he and his brothers are working in the field binding sheaves of wheat. "Behold my sheaf rose and stood straight," Yosef recounts for his brothers, "and your sheaves

Rabbi Balkany is dean of the Bais Yaakov of Brooklyn, New York.

encircled and bowed to my sheaf" (*Bereishis* 37:7). Yosef's description of his superiority elicits his brothers' resentment.

Yosef then has a second dream. "Behold the sun, moon and eleven stars are bowing to me," he relates to his father and brothers. This time it is Yaakov who reacts angrily to the inherent symbolism. "What is this dream you have dreamed? Will I and your mother and brothers come and bow to the ground before you?" (37:10).

Yaakov's reaction is odd in light of his personal history. Was not his own life immeasurably influenced by dreams? After leaving his parents' home, he dreamt about a ladder carrying angels between the heavens and earth; then G-d appeared to him and promised to be his guide. Later, in a dream he had while working for Lavan, G-d showed Yaakov the way to attain prosperity. Then He ordered Yaakov to leave his father-in-law's house and return to the land of Canaan. After these seminal experiences — all prefaced by dreams — how could Yaakov dismiss his son's dreams out of hand?

Indeed, he does not. Immediately after Yaakov criticizes Yosef, it is written, "And his father guarded the situation" (37:11). His outward display of anger belied an inner conviction that these dreams were more than mere youthful imagination. "[Yaakov] waited and watched for when it would come [true]," Rashi notes.

And come true it did — but not for a long time, time filled with all sorts of trouble for Yosef. He is captured by his brothers, thrown into a pit of snakes and scorpions, and then sold to a caravan of Yishmaelites travelling to Egypt. In Egypt, he is again sold as a slave to Potiphar, an officer in Pharaoh's court. There, "G-d is with Yosef, and he becomes a successful man" (39:2).

Suddenly and inexplicably, Yosef's fortunes are reversed when he is accused by Potiphar's wife of disloyalty and immediately jailed in Pharaoh's dungeon. Yosef is unjustly stripped of his position, his freedom, his contact with the outside world. Nevertheless, the Torah writes, "G-d is with Yosef" (39:21). In the next *parshah,* Yosef is released from prison after interpreting Pharaoh's dreams and is quickly appointed viceroy over all of Egypt.

Dreams play a major role in Yosef's destiny. After many long and hard years his prophetic dreams are fulfilled, culminating in his reunion with his father.

None of this could have been predicted at the start of the *parshah,* which opens innocently enough: "And Yaakov dwelled (*Vayeishev*) in the land in which his fathers lived, the land of Canaan" (37:1). But Rashi, examining the word *vayeishev*, quotes the Midrash: "Yaakov wished to dwell in harmony . . . .G-d said, 'Is [the reward] reserved for the righteous in the World to Come not enough that they also wish to dwell in harmony in this world?!'" Immediately, Yosef is taken away from him. It is a haunting Midrash.

Yaakov's dream featured a ladder that extended from the earth to the heavens with angels descending to and returning from their missions. Yosef's dreams also began on earth and ended in the heavens. But until he was able to see those dreams come to a fruition of heaven-sent goodness, he had to take a long and arduous journey and climb beyond the rungs of despair.

My dear *chassan* and *kallah,* the lives of our ancestors provide us, their descendants, with valuable lessons. At no point in your lives are you as full of hopes and dreams as you are today at the start of your marriage. You should both be dreaming of success and happiness. But in order to achieve these often elusive goals, you must have a ladder of *bitachon* to bring your aspirations heavenward. You must continually recognize that it may take time to realize your dreams. Nevertheless, through it all, the good and less-than-good times, G-d will be with you as He was with our ancestor, Yosef. Your mission is to continually strive for all that is good and holy. May your lives together, lived in accordance with the Torah, bring you happiness from above. May all your prayers be answered and your dreams turned into reality.

Rabbi Louis Bernstein

פרשת מקץ
Parshas Mikeitz

REAMS ARE A PRECIOUS COMMODITY. For a young, newly
married couple the whole future is mapped out in
dreams.

Although the last four books of the *Chumash* do not record any
dreams, the book of *Bereishis* is the book of dreams. After taking Sarah
away from Avraham, Avimelech, king of Gerar, is warned by G-d in a
dream (*Bereishis* 20:3). Yaakov, while dreaming of angels ascending and
descending a ladder that stretches from heaven to earth, receives a
promise from G-d that his children will inherit the Holy Land (28:12).
Yosef dreams first of sheaves (37:5), then of stars (37:9) — dreams which
cause discord between him and his brothers and lead to his sale into
slavery. Then in Egypt, Yosef is thrown in jail where he meets two of
Pharaoh's officers, both of whom dream of their fates (40:5).

And in *Parshas Mikeitz*, Pharaoh himself dreams.

In his dream, the Egyptian monarch is standing at the bank of the Nile.
The Torah records his location because of its symbolism: To this day the

---

*Rabbi Bernstein, of blessed memory, was rav of the Young Israel of Windsor Park
in Bayside, New York.*

Nile is responsible for all of Egypt's agriculture, and, in ancient times, the river was treated as a deity. The Egyptians did not just depend on the Nile, they worshipped it.

Pharaoh's dream centered around cows and grain rising up out of the river and devouring each other. He could not understand the meaning behind the strange dreams and called upon his advisors to unravel their mystery. But none helped him. Not that they didn't understand their meaning, our Sages explain. They were able to decipher what the dreams signified and what was in store for their country, but they were unwilling to reveal this information to their king. They recognized the bad news portended by the dreams and preferred to leave the unpleasant task of reporting it to Pharaoh in the hands of the prisoner-interpreter, Yosef.

The truths these dreams revealed shattered their perception of the Nile as a god, for if it was a god, why would it fail them? If, as they believed, their god existed to serve them, to irrigate their fields and provide food and water for them, why would it turn against them? Why would their god subject them to seven years of famine? To their way of thinking, it was all so incomprehensible. Their concept of a god who serves Egypt left no room for the possibility of a god who judges them.

The Egyptians' attitude toward higher powers is alluded to in the *parshah's* first verse, describing Pharaoh's dream: "Behold, he is standing over the river" (*Bereishis* 41:1). The Torah is telling us more than Pharaoh's physical location on the bank of the Nile; it describes his state of mind. He sees himself as master over the river — standing atop nature. It is nature and, by extension, the deities that run nature, which are subject to man's whims, not vice versa.

But this is not the Jew's view of the world. When Yaakov dreams of the ladder, he sees more than angels. "And behold, G-d stood above him" (28:13). Yaakov's perspective is clear: G-d stands atop him and it is his job to serve G-d. Man is subject to G-d's desires, man must accept the yoke of heaven, not the other way around (*Bereishis Rabbah* 89:4).

Pharaoh and all Egyptians felt the Nile was under their control, subject to their needs and desires. It was strange to them that the river would turn against them.

The content of Pharaoh's dream is also instructive. The lean cows devoured the fat cows — this can be understood in two ways: Rashi understands that the years of famine would overwhelm the years of plenty to the point that the years of plenty would be forgotten. Yosef, therefore, advised Pharaoh to store enough grain to insure this would not happen. The Ramban, on the other hand, understands Yosef's advice as being inherent in the dream itself — the years of famine would be neutralized by the years of plenty, just as the lean cows were nourished by the fat cows.

Marriage can also be seen in this dichotomy. Marriage is a lifelong commitment and along life's bumpy road there are good times and there are bad times. A couple can either allow the bad times to overwhelm the good times; when difficulties come along, they can forget the positive moments. Or they can take a more productive route and follow Yosef's advice. Allow the times of famine to feed off the years of plenty. During troubled times, recall the good parts of life and be nourished from them.

Furthermore, a Jewish couple's dreams are not just their own; they are *Klal Yisrael's* dreams. "And Pharaoh dreamed." The Midrash points out that in the Hebrew vernacular the verb always precedes the noun, except when the *pasuk* wants to place special emphasis on the noun, as it does here — *"U'Pharaoh choleim."* Why the special emphasis on Pharaoh? Because, explains the Midrash, a king's dream affects his entire nation. The *pasuk* spotlights Pharaoh; this is no ordinary Egyptian dreaming.

So too our Sages state, *"Chassan domeh lemelech* — A bridegroom is like a king" (*Pirkei deRebbi Eliezer* 16). The dreams of a newly married couple are not theirs alone; they belong to the whole nation.

My dear *chassan* and *kallah,* young couples must have beautiful dreams of the future, both material and spiritual. But these dreams will only be realized through the recognition that *"Hashem nitzav alav,"* that G-d stands atop you. Our Jewish future, to which you add another important edifice, depends on your dreams.

The Gemara in *Berachos* (55b) states that all dreams follow their interpretation. We know your dreams will be noble and holy. By accepting the task of serving G-d and glorifying His Name, you will assume the greatest role a person, a couple, a family can play on this world — bringing G-dliness to our planet, as the ladder in Yaakov's dream linked heaven and earth. In this way you will secure for yourselves blessings here and in the world to come.

Rabbi Herzel Kranz

ONE OF THE UNIQUE EXPRESSIONS and concepts in Judaism is found when a couple marries and the *chassan* and *kallah* are referred to as a king and queen. Is this simply a beautiful thought, part of the blessing we bestow upon the couple on the most important day of their lives, or does it signify something more tangible? What is the real meaning of this comparison to royalty?

Parshas Mikeitz records in detail the dreams of Pharaoh. He craved to know what those dreams meant, seeking from his advisors the meaning behind the seven fat cows and the seven lean cows, the seven healthy sheaves and the seven blighted sheaves. All the interpretations given to him, state the commentaries, were of a personal nature, and they did not satisfy Pharaoh.

It was then that Yosef, the Jewish lad, was released from prison to give his interpretation of the dreams, and what he had to say, Pharaoh accepted. The dreams signified a national crisis, but one that could be

Rabbi Kranz is rav of the Silver Spring Jewish Center in Silver Spring, Maryland.

averted with the proper planning. Yosef was then appointed viceroy of Egypt and put in charge of implementing this seven-year plan, and the course of Jewish history was forever changed.

How did Pharaoh know that Yosef's vision was correct? Why did he accept the word of a young, foreign prisoner?

Wise Pharaoh understood that he was always occupied with Egypt's national affairs, not personal matters. If his waking time was spent in this frame of mind then his sleeping time would surely reflect that as well. If Yosef's interpretation of the dreams were correct, every Egyptian man, woman and child would be affected by the coming famine and by Pharaoh's response to it. Thus, his conscience was rested after hearing Yosef's words.

In a like manner, when a young couple decide to get married, both continue to have their own particular needs and desires. But each is more concerned with the material and emotional burdens that come with undertaking the new and challenging responsibilities that come with marriage. From this point on, their concerns will be broader, less personal, encompassing spouse, family and community.

A couple standing under the *chuppah* are like Adam and Chavah at the dawn of civilization, from whom all humanity descended. Each couple is unique and stands at the beginning of the process of building a whole new world. The thoughts of *chassan* and *kallah,* therefore, transcend the mundane matters surrounding them and concern the kingdom and world they now set out to fashion. Accordingly, their family and friends shower them with the respect and honor, the pomp and circumstance reserved for royalty.

My dear *chassan* and *kallah,* you remain today in our presence as king and queen. We wish for you that your dreams for building your world together meet only with success and happiness, securing for yourselves a prominent place in the history of our nation.

Rabbi Mark Nenner

פרשת ויגש
Parshas Vayigash

T HE SAGA OF YOSEF AND HIS BROTHERS is a story for the ages, containing all the elements of human drama. Sibling rivalry, jealousy and temptation are but a few of the threads the Torah weaves together as it tells this incredible tale, a tale full of emotion and complete with a powerful ending. Yosef is alive and well and living as viceroy of Egypt. The destiny of *Klal Yisrael* unfolds through the hidden working of G-d's hand — a remarkable finish to a tumultuous journey.

The Torah tells us that when Yosef's brothers told their father the good news, "*Vatichi ruach Yaakov avihem*, And the spirit of their father, Yaakov, was revived" (*Bereishis* 45:27). Rashi explains this verse to mean that Yaakov was more than happy; he was transformed — the *Shechinah* returned to him after 22 years. One can only imagine the emotional impact on a man who, as a result of a tragedy, lost his Divine

---

Rabbi Nenner is educational director of the Holliswood Jewish Center in Holliswood, New York and director of New York Junior N.C.S.Y.

inspiration. Surely the revelation of Yosef's survival was an incredible event.

What is puzzling, however, is Yosef's behavior throughout this ordeal. Surely he knew his father was suffering. Why did he not inform him of his whereabouts? Certainly once he ascended to royalty he could have notified him. Why wasn't Yosef worried about his father? What right did he have to prolong his father's agony and withhold from him the joy that was *"vatichi ruach Yaakov avihem"*?

The *Or Hachaim* solves this enigma with a dual approach. First, there was a Divine plan at work here which precluded Yaakov from knowing the true fate of his son. Our Sages explain that Yaakov was sentenced from Above to 22 years of parental anguish for the 22 years he spent away from home, unavailable to serve his parents. A revelation of Yosef's whereabouts would have voided this Divine retribution.

This approach explains G-d's rationale for keeping Yosef's secret. What it fails to address, however, is Yosef's angle. One must find justification for Yosef's action from a perspective of human nature and free will.

The *Or Hachaim*, therefore, offers another, more practical, explanation. Yosef's silence was indeed justified, for it reflected a decision based on logistics, sensitivity and good judgment. When Yosef was a slave, communication with his father was outside his realm of ability. And even if he had gotten the chance to send a message, he feared retribution from his brothers, as they would no doubt be castigated or even cursed by their father for what they had done to him.

Later, once he had ascended to royalty and was more at ease about his safety, Yosef could have told the tale. But he still had a reason to stay quiet, for he did not want to embarrass his brothers, in accordance with the dictum, "Better a person should throw himself into a fiery furnace and not shame his friend" (*Berachos* 43b). Because humiliating someone is tantamount to killing him, Yosef decided that elongating Yaakov's pain was the lesser of two evils: better to keep quiet than to expose a scandal in the Patriarchal dynasty.

Only after Yosef fed his brothers and gave them money, only after he dealt with them in good faith, could he make his startling revelation. Once his brothers saw he had no hard feelings toward them, once he impressed upon them *"ki lemichyah shelachani Elokim"* (45:5) — that he had been at the center of a Divine plan — their humiliation was tempered as well as their potential anger and retribution.

Yosef's silence, one sees, was justified; it was all a matter of timing. As great as was the need to ease his father's pain, the consideration of all these other factors superseded that need.

We live in a world of many mystifying events. Tragedies, difficulties, pain and sorrow are often along the walkway of *Klal Yisrael's* destiny. Yet, through it all, we as Jews believe *"Kol mah de'avid Rachmana letav avid"* (*Berachos* 60b). Everything G-d does He does for our benefit and with our best interests in mind. What *we* must keep in mind is that we are not privy to G-d's sense of timing.

Yes, there will be good in the world, there will be a redemption, there will be an end to our pain and suffering — all in its proper time. There are details we may not be aware of, details only G-d is aware of, details that are necessary for the desired outcome.

My dear *chassan* and *kallah,* as you sit together before us today, you are living testimony to G-d's remarkable sense of timing. Both of you have been through the rigors of dating, through the pain of false hope and disappointment of previous relationships, through the difficult ordeal of being without a mate. When, you wondered, would your relief come? Why was G-d withholding your *zivug*, your life's partner? Why were you not able to experience *"vatechi ruach,"* an uplifting of your spirit?

Nonetheless, you always knew in the back of your minds that Hashem would deliver, that He would end your suffering. You knew He had a plan, but that it was subject to the proper timing. Only after the pain and anguish of searching for your mate impacted on your characters and helped define who you were and what you were looking for, only then could you appreciate the grace of G-d and the gift He has given both of you. May G-d bless you with everything in its proper time and may you grow to appreciate each other more and more, just as you appreciate the powerful workings of the A-mighty.

Rabbi Aryeh Weil

פרשת ויחי
Parshas Vayechi

U NDER THE *CHUPPAH,* both *chassan* and *kallah* wear white. The *kallah* wears her gown and the *chassan* dons a *kittel* over his suit. Contained in these clothes is a dual symbolism, signifying, on the one hand, purity and majesty in honor of the occasion, and, at the same time, serving as a reminder of the simple white clothes the *kohein gadol* wore as he performed the Yom Kippur service, begging G-d's forgiveness for the entire Jewish people. The young couple, too, ask G-d for forgiveness on this day, their personal Yom Kippur, their white clothing providing an atmosphere of solemnity and reflection during these precious moments.

These two notions, majesty and solemnity, are captured in a pair of markedly different words that are often coupled together: *chessed* and *emes*. *Chessed* — literally "breaking the bounds," transcending that which is normal — is found at a wedding, which uplifts its participants from the standard routine of life. *Emes* — a more rigid concept, the cold, logical truth — is also found on the wedding day, as *chassan* and *kallah* confess their past sins to the Creator.

Rabbi Weil is dean of students at Yeshivat Ohr Yerushalayim in Jerusalem.

These two terms, *chessed* and *emes*, are voiced by Yaakov as he is about to die. In *Parshas Vayechi* he calls for his son, Yosef, and asks him to "act toward me with kindness and truth; do not bury me in Egypt" (*Bereishis* 47:29). Kindness, *chessed*, is a cornerstone of Jewish living, yet more elusive than one might think. Only once someone has died, our Sages say, can kindness truly be dealt. Why? Because when doing a favor, it is within human nature to expect something in return. Even if no explicit request is made, there always remains an implicit contract. It is hard to refuse someone who once helped you; you always "owe him one."

But when someone is dead, he can offer no recompense. For this reason only members of a Jewish community's ritual burial society are considered capable of performing *chessed shel emes*, kindness in its truest form, as they prepare the deceased for burial and escort him to the grave. This was Yaakov's request.

With this definition in mind, it is surprising to discover in the Torah other instances of the pairing of *chessed* with *emes* which do not deal with burial. When Eliezer asks Rivkah's father and brother for permission to marry her to Yitzchak, he says, "And now, if you are willing to deal in kindness and truth with my master, tell me" (*Bereishis* 24:49).

Another instance is found in the story of the spies who went to Yericho in the time of Yehoshua. They were safely hidden by a woman named Rachav and promised her that "when G-d gives us the land, we will deal with you in kindness and truth" (*Yehoshua* 2:14). How is one to understand these examples of kindness and truth which are not in the context of burial?

The *Sifsei Chachamim* acknowledges that these examples demonsrate the possibility of acting with both kindness and truth even during one's lifetime. How does one achieve this? By dismissing any possibility of reciprocation. Then, even the living can perform acts of kindness in their truest, purest form.

This is the challenge every couple faces entering marriage: To create the oneness that is a marriage, true kindness must be enacted. All acts of kindness between spouses must be done selflessly with no thought of return. Done in this manner, every act of kindness strengthens the union.

Truth in kindness also suggests that the ideal state of practicing kindness emanates from a sense of truth. *Emes* demands that one practice *chessed*. "The world is built upon kindness," declared the Psalmist (89:3). And: "Whoever renounces kindness is considered to have renounced the essence" of Judaism (*Koheles Rabbah* 7:4). And: "There is no limit to acts of kindness" (*Pei'ah* 1:1), which can be understood to mean that opportunities to do kindness abound, and also that every individual act of kindness is immeasurable.

The realities of marriage run parallel to the realities of life, so that marriage, too, demands kindness to insure success. The merging of two people, two personalities is such that it requires some leeway, some giving from each party in order for the union to take root and to flourish. It is that very kindness and compromise that also makes marriage so valuable and productive.

My dear *chassan* and *kallah,* the ability to give freely and regularly is a fundamental ingredient in every marriage. Both of you come into this union having been reared in homes suffused with kindness and the values of our Torah. It is now your turn to insure that your home is built upon the same elementary qualities. First, kindness must flow from each of you without regard for return from the other. Then you must expand that attitude to include your community and your people, opening your home to guests, your wallet to the poor, and your schedule to meaningful causes. In this manner you will fashion for yourselves a faithful home in Israel and establish yourselves as invaluable members of G-d's chosen nation.

◄§ *Sefer Shemos*

Rabbi Jacob J. Schacter

פרשת שמות
Parshas Shemos

THE SECOND BIBLICAL BOOK BEGINS: "These are the names of the children of Israel who came to Egypt" (*Shemos* 1:1), and, in keeping with the custom of naming every *parshah* and book of the *Chumash* by reference to one of its opening words, this book is called *Shemos*, Names. In English, however, it carries a title that reflects the major theme of the *parshah* as a whole — Exodus, the Jews' miraculous redemption from slavery and their departure from Egypt.

These two titles, though, are intimately linked in the Midrash. "Rabbi Huna said in the name of Bar Kapara: For four reasons Israel was redeemed from Egypt. First, because they did not change their names..." (*Shemos Rabbah* 1:28). The names Jewish parents gave their children — Jewish names and not Egyptian names — were a major factor in ultimately making possible the exodus. By keeping their Jewish names, the children of Israel preserved their identity and protected their destiny as God's chosen nation.

Rabbi Schacter is rav of The Jewish Center in New York City.

The story of that destiny begins with Moshe venturing out of the king's palace, the home of Pharaoh, where he grew up. The Torah describes how he "went out" into the world of his Jewish brethren, coming face to face for the first time with their tragic plight. "And he saw an Egyptian striking a Hebrew, from his brothers. And he turned this way and that" — Moshe looked into his future, explains Rashi, and saw nothing worth saving — "and he struck the Egyptian," killing him (2:11-12).

"With what did he kill him?" asks the Midrash (*Shemos Rabbah* 1:29) and, in response, lists three opinions. "Rabbi Evyasar says, he hit him with his fist; others say, he took a clay tool and bludgeoned him; and the Rabbanan say, he invoked the Name [of God] against him and killed him."

This last scenario is the one incorporated by Rashi into his commentary: "He killed him with the *Shem Hameforash*," with God's secret, mystical, ineffable Name (2:14). According to this interpretation, it is apparent that Moshe was familiar with the *Shem Hameforash*.

With this in mind, it is odd that, several verses later, when confronted by God at the burning bush and ordered to return to Egypt to begin his historic mission, Moshe asks God, "When I will come to the children of Israel and say to them, 'The God of your fathers has sent me to you,' and they ask me, 'What is His name?' — what shall I say to them?" (*Shemos* 3:13). If, as the Midrash and Rashi contend, Moshe knew the Name of God well enough to invoke its awesome power, what was the basis for his current question?

The *Sefas Emes* notes that God does not have only one Name but many Names. True, Moshe knew the *Shem* that can be used for destruction, which, when invoked, can kill someone, and he utilized it successfully. But a different *Shem* would need to be employed to bring about redemption, to elevate a people from the depths of slavery and spiritual poverty and deliver them to freedom and moral purpose. This was the *Shem* that Moshe sought at the burning bush. This was the *Shem* that Moshe needed to bring to the Benei Yisrael to impress upon them the imminence of the exodus. This *Shem* was unknown to Moshe and so He was compelled to ask God to share it with him.

This distinction between God's various Names reflects a powerful message. How often throughout human history has God's Name been invoked for murder and destruction? How many Jews have been killed by non-Jews over the centuries — in the name of God. Religious extremists use violence to terrorize and kill people, including their fellow citizens — all in the name of God. Even within our own community, Jews attack, vilify, degrade and even kill other Jews — again in the name of God.

This Name of God — horribly misused and distorted — is very well known. But our task in life is, as Moshe's was, to learn the other Name of God, to learn the Name that unites us, the Name that brings peace and redemption. We must use God's Name for positive purposes, to grow, to build up ourselves and our nation.

My dear *chassan* and *kallah,* how fortunate you are that you and your families understand and appreciate the example of the positive *Shem Hameforash*. God has granted you great qualities and abilities — an appreciation for Torah and its study, a sensitivity to the need for charity and kindness, great intelligence which has allowed you to reach significant heights in your chosen fields of interest, and a sense of communal responsibility — all of which you both have learned from your respective parental homes. You know what it means to act positively and constructively for the benefit of the Jewish people, and to do so reflecting the Name of God.

May you build a genuine Jewish home that will sanctify God's Name and be a source of pride for yourselves, your family and all of *Klal Yisrael.*

Rabbi Walter Wurzburger

פרשת וארא
Parshas Va'eira

W HEN MAN AND WOMAN STAND under the *chuppah* to become husband and wife, they begin together a life that surpasses the individual lives they led until that moment, for one who is unmarried, our Sages declare, is considered incomplete.

There is a word in *Parshas Va'eira* that provides an invaluable insight into the purpose of a Jewish marriage. After delivering the Jews from Egypt, G-d promises to bring them into Eretz Yisrael, stating, "I will give her to you as a *morashah*" (*Shemos* 6:8).

This word, *morashah*, is used in only one other place in the *Chumash*, when the Torah is described as "*morashah kehillas Yaakov*" (*Devarim* 33:4). The *Baal Haturim* contrasts this word with the word *yerushah*; the difference in spelling is slight, but important. Both indicate a form of inheritance; but unlike a *yerushah*, a *morashah* does not transfer automatically. The word is proactive — a *morashah* requires effort.

Rabbi Wurzburger is rabbi emeritus of Congregation Shaarei Tefila in Lawrence, New York.

The mishnah in *Avos* (6:6) enumerates the hardships one must endure in order to achieve excellence in Torah study. Likewise, the Holy Land is acquired only through adversity (*Berachos* 5a). This is the quality of a *morashah* — it is obtained only with special effort.

Furthermore, our Sages maintain a connection between the word *morashah* and a phonetically similar word, *me'orasah*, one who is betrothed (*Berachos* 57a). There is a connection between a *morashah* and a marriage. This comparison is telling. To succeed in marriage, a couple must view it as a *morashah*. They need to understand that the development of a relationship requires effort. They must never take each other for granted and must continually make efforts to be responsive to each other's needs. For their marriage to succeed, they must avoid turning it into a routine and instead strive to build an inspiring relationship.

Moreover, their marriage must incorporate the *morashah* of Torah. A successful Jewish family life is dependent on it being patterned in accordance with the Torah's guidelines. A home where Torah is studied and mitzvos are observed is a home that is blessed with the spirit of G-d.

It is well known that on the day of their wedding, a *chassan* and *kallah* are absolved from all their sins. Why should this be so? What is so extraordinary about getting married that it is rewarded with the erasure of one's entire record of sin?

The Talmud Yerushalmi lists several people whose circumstances cause their slate to be wiped clean: a bridegroom; a scholar who is appointed to a post of communal responsibility; a person elevated to a position of political leadership; and a non-Jew who converts to Judaism. All of these people share a common denominator. Each, by virtue of his new responsibilities, undergoes changes that transform him into a new person. Once considered a new person, the sins of his past are, technically, no longer his.

A *chassan* becomes truly a new person because marriage calls for the ability to transcend the narrow confines of individualism and commit one's whole self to another person. As long as one is single, the tendency is to be self-centered, the primary concern is self-fulfillment. After marriage, one understands that "It is not good for man to be alone" (*Bereishis* 2:18). The realization that "his wife is like his own self" (*Berachos* 24a) is the first step in a process of liberation from the confines of self-centeredness, extending the range of one's vision to encompass solicitude for others.

A Jewish home is not a castle shutting out the outside world. At the entrances of Jewish homes are *mezuzos*, not "do not disturb" signs. This impresses upon their occupants their responsibilities to others, the advice of Yosai ben Yochanan in *Avos* (1:5) to "let your home be wide open" to offer comfort to others. The harmony and peace prevailing within a Jewish family should not be treated as a haven to escape from one's responsibilities toward the world. The sense of attachment that the Torah mandates to spouses should generate a broader love and concern for one's community, nation and all humanity.

The *me'orasah-morashah* equation provides another vital lesson: In marriage, one's concern must not be limited to the present. Jews, as custodians of a *morashah* that must be passed from generation to generation, shoulder a great responsibility for the future. Jews, therefore, need to continually ask themselves whether their lifestyle and value system is conducive to bequeathing to their children and grandchildren a love of Torah and commitment to Eretz Yisrael. The success of a marriage is gauged not only by the measure of devotion cultivated for one another, but also by the degree to which one has successfully transmitted the *morashah* that has been entrusted to the Jewish people.

My dear *chassan* and *kallah,* Rabbeinu Bechayeh writes that a marriage is a re-enactment of Creation. Just as the creation of the universe took seven days, we celebrate a new marriage for seven days. Your parents, families and friends rejoice with you at this magnificent moment, the creation of your new world. We pray that the establishment of your Torah home will bring *Klal Yisrael* closer to the ideals of our *morashah* and to the ultimate redemption of all humanity.

Rabbi Menachem Genack

פרשת וארא
Parshas Va'eira

J UST BEFORE THE *CHASSAN* PUTS THE RING on the *kallah's* finger, the officiating rabbi says the *berachah* praising G-d "Who sanctifies His nation, Israel, through the nuptial canopy (*chuppah*) and marital consecration (*kiddushin*)."

A Jewish marriage consists of two distinct components: *erusin* and *nessuin*. *Erusin*, also called *kiddushin*, is the first stage and serves as the official, legal betrothal of woman to man. When the *kallah* accepts the ring from the chassan, *erusin* is accomplished.

The second stage is *nessuin*. The Gemara defines *nessuin* simply as *chuppah*. What *chuppah* is exactly is the center of much debate among the Rishonim, the halachic decisors of the Middle Ages. In order to achieve *chuppah* in accordance with as many of these opinions as possible, a variety of rituals are observed. One of them, the nuptial canopy under which *chassan* and *kallah* stand, has been singled out for the term *chuppah*. That is, by doing nothing more than standing under this special canopy, the couple carries out *nessuin*.

The distinction between *erusin* and *nessuin* is blurred these days because both take place almost simultaneously, with the couple arriving under the canopy moments before the ring is given; as soon as *erusin* takes place, the couple is already positioned for *nessuin*. But in generations past, these two events occurred at different times. The couple would become halachically bound to each other through *erusin* weeks or even months before the wedding celebration and *nessuin* would take place. At those times it was clear that *erusin* came first. Why then did the Sages prescribe a blessing that inverts the order, placing *nessuin* (*chuppah*) ahead of *erusin* (*kiddushin*)?

Another oddity lies in the text of the *berachah*: How does G-d sanctify Israel through *chuppah* and *kiddushin*? How is the holiness of the Jewish people contingent upon the institution of marriage?

To understand the wording of this *berachah*, one must be familiar with the first Jewish wedding — a marriage not between man and woman but between G-d and the Jewish people. "And I shall take you to me as a nation" (*Shemos* 6:7), G-d tells Moshe regarding the Israelites before redeeming them from Egypt. G-d then fulfilled his promise when he gave the Jewish nation the Torah.

At Sinai, G-d lifted the mountain over the Jewish people before offering them the Torah. This was their *chuppah*. Then G-d presented them with the *Shenei Luchos Habris*, the Two Tablets of the Covenant. This was their *kiddushin*. At the marriage of G-d and his nation, *chuppah* came before *kiddushin*. This is the wedding, explains the Maharsha, that is referred to in the *berachah* pronounced at every subsequent Jewish wedding.

This *berachah* links every contemporary celebration to the quintessential moment in Jewish history. Husband and wife are not only joined to each other; their commitment recalls that time in history when the Jews accepted the Torah. Each new marriage merges the commitment of a newly married couple with the historic drama of Sinai.

The ability of the wedding ceremony to transcend personal joy and take on national significance is the reason why a glass is broken at the conclusion of the ceremony. This is done to honor the memory of the destroyed Temple. A couple must be reminded, even at the most precious moment of their personal lives, that their role as Jews, seen in a national context, in the stream of Jewish history, finds them in exile, removed from the close relationship with G-d that was firmly established when the Temple stood.

My dear *chassan* and *kallah,* by intimately tying your wedding to the history of the Jewish people you have signified that your marriage will strive to further the destiny of the Jewish people. By building a Jewish home based on the precepts of Sinai, a home that reflects your commitment to G-d, His Torah and His commandments, you evince your love for G-d and pave the way for the restoration of His monarchy and His Temple.

Rabbi Avraham Mandelbaum

פרשת בא
Parshas Bo

A FTER THE *CHASSAN* PLACES THE RING on the finger of his beloved *kallah,* the two witnesses announce *"Mekudeshes* — She is consecrated." The same declaration is found in connection with the *mitzvah* of *kiddush hachodesh*, the sanctification of the new month. After accepting testimony from witnesses that a new moon was seen in the skies, the Beis Din would announce, *"Mekudash* — It is sanctified," thus beginning a new month.

These two pronouncements of *kiddush* are linked in another way. The first *mitzvah* recorded in the Torah is that of *"Peru urevu,"* the command to procreate, which is the ultimate responsibility of a Jewish union. But the first *mitzvah* given to the Jewish people as a nation is *"Hachodesh hazeh lachem rosh chadashim"* (*Shemos* 12:2) — the mitzvah of *kiddush hachodesh*. The Torah could have begun with this *pasuk,* the first Rashi in *Chumash* points out.

Moreover, both the marriage ceremony and the establishment of the new month share two characteristics: *kiddush* and *chiddush* —

Rabbi Mandelbaum is rav of Congregation Ahavas Yisroel in Hewlett, New York.

consecration and renewal, two themes that are indispensable to Judaism. Rav Avraham Yitzchak Hakohein Kook, the first Chief Rabbi of Israel, encapsulated these two themes, stating that the Jewish mission in Eretz Yisrael was *"Lechadeish es hayashan, velekadeish es hechadash* — To renew the old, and to consecrate the new."

These words are the secret to Jewish survival. The ability of the Jewish people to maintain their beautiful, venerable, holy traditions throughout the centuries has kept our nation timely, vital and vigorous. *Lechadeish es hayashan*. The observance of each generation of Torah Jews renews an ancient mandate.

Simultaneously, Jews are responsible *lekadeish es hachadash*. New times bring new challenges and new opportunities, which must also find their place in the world of Torah. Advancements in technology and communication provide us with tools to advance Jewish causes. Our nation, which has always had to adapt to new situations and circumstances, welcomes these new opportunities into the "four cubits of halachah." Thus, the new becomes consecrated.

Rav Joseph B. Soloveitchik drives this point home in his classic work, *Halakhic Man*, in which he contrasts "halachic man" with the universal *homo religiosus*, or "religious man." While religious man seeks to escape the mundane world, a world of blandishments and lurid temptations, in search of the pure, ethereal domain of the Divine, the halachic man single-mindedly devotes himself to sanctifying the material world, suffusing it with purpose, dignity and holiness, bringing G-d into the world of the five senses.

This *kiddush* is coupled with the continual cycle of *chiddush*. The Midrash (*Pesikta Rabbasi* 15) likens the Jewish people to the moon, and the Jewish calendar follows a lunar schedule. The fate of the Jewish nation, says the Midrash, waxes and wanes like the moon. Shlomo Hamelech reigned in Jerusalem fifteen generations after Avraham Avinu lived, corresponding to the fifteenth day of the month, when the moon is full. Fifteen generations later, corresponding to the end of the month, when the moon is dark, Tzidkiyahu Hamelech was exiled by Nevuchadnetzar.

Just as the moon renews itself each month, the Jewish people are challenged to regularly renew themselves and their commitment to G-d. The *pasuk* states: "On this day the L-rd, your G-d, commands you to do" the *mitzvos* (*Devarim* 26:16), to which Rashi notes, "Every day they should be in your eyes as new, as if they were commanded on that day." In order for Torah and Judaism to be continually meaningful and relevant, one must view them through the element of *chiddush*. This notion is amplified in the blessing said both before and after the reading of the Torah, when we bless G-d "Who *gives* the Torah." We must perpetually feel that the Torah is being given to us in the here and now.

My dear *chassan* and *kallah,* may you bring into your marriage these two lofty ideals, *chiddush* and *kiddush*. As you build your Jewish home, view every day of your life together through the prism of renewal and consecration. Renew your commitment, faith, love and devotion to each other every day. Do not allow your marriage to become stale and antiquated.

As you share new experiences together, remember to infuse them with *kedushah*. Do not be afraid to face new challenges, to uncover new horizons, to embark on new voyages. Allow the compass of *kedushah* to navigate you through unchartered waters and turn them into spiritual waters. May G-d fortify you with these two spiritual moorings and may your home be a place where the A-mighty is forever present.

Rabbi Avromy Fein

פרשת בשלח
Parshas Beshalach

P
ARSHAS BESHALACH CONTAINS the famous episode of Amaleik's attack upon the Jewish nation just after they left Egypt under G-d's protection. The timing of this incident was no coincidence, states the Midrash, for immediately preceding Amaleik's attack, the Jews, complaining about the lack of water in the wilderness, asked, "Is G-d in our midst or not?" (*Shemos* 17:7). This reaction came just after G-d split the Red Sea and led them through it and after G-d began providing them with the manna that sustained them throughout their journey.

To what is this compared? asks Rabbi Levi in the Midrash (*Tanchuma*, *Yisro* 3). To a child who is riding on his father's shoulders. When the child sees something he wants, he asks his father for it and his father gets it for him. This happens again and again. Then they encounter another person and the child asks this stranger, "Have you seen my father?" The father responds incredulously, "You ride on my shoulders and everything you want I get you, yet you ask, 'Have you seen my

---

Rabbi Fein is a practicing attorney in Monsey, New York.

father?'" The father then takes him down from his shoulders and a dog comes and bites the child.

Likewise, the Jewish people displayed unimaginable impudence in asking the very same question, "Is G-d in our midst or not?" How could they doubt G-d's fidelity when He had just delivered them from slavery in Egypt?

G-d's response was swift and harsh: "And Amaleik came and warred with Israel at Refidim" (17:8). A previous *pasuk* already mentioned that they were camped at Refidim, but the Torah repeats their location, says the *Sifsei Chachamim*, because their behavior at Refidim is what brought about the war. By daring to ask if G-d was with them when it was clear He was leading them, the Jewish people invited attack upon themselves. G-d cast Amaleik upon the Jewish people as a not-so-gentle reminder that a sense of appreciation is basic in any relationship.

Appreciating G-d's generosity is a theme found in all the Jewish holidays. The Talmud states, "When Adar approaches, joy increases" (*Taanis* 29a). What is it about the imminence of Adar that increases joy? Adar, notes Rashi, brings with it the miraculous days of Purim and Pesach, two holidays that serve to remind the Jewish people of G-d's benevolence.

The debt of gratitude Jews owe to the Creator, observes Rav Chaim Yaakov Goldvicht, is noted in the first of the Ten Commandments: "I am the L-rd, your G-d, Who took you out from the land of Egypt" (*Shemos* 20:2). The Jewish people's responsibility toward G-d is connected to G-d's redeeming them from Egypt. Our obligation to accept the yoke of Torah is inherent in our appreciation of the goodness G-d has bestowed upon us throughout history. The more Jews are cognizant of G-d's goodness, the more we are obligated to serve Him.

But because the Jewish people lacked this elementary recognition and they remained doubtful in the face of all this evidence, G-d let loose Amaleik upon them. The battle awakened within them the realization of how vulnerable they were without G-d's protection. For this reason we read this section, *Parshas Zachor*, each year before Purim. By retelling the battle of Amaleik, we regularly remind ourselves to be appreciative.

This same lesson is then repeated on Pesach, at the *seder,* with the reading of the Haggadah, an annual recollection of past events, that G-d redeemed us from Egypt, gave us the Torah, and led us into the Promised Land.

The Torah once again conveys the message of the need for gratitude in the juxtaposition of two seemingly dissimilar ideas: the bringing of sacrifices by the tribal leaders at the end of *Parshas Naso* and the *mitzvah* of lighting the Menorah at the start of *Parshas Behaalosecha*. Our Sages wonder: What links these two?

The Midrash relates that Aharon was dismayed that his tribe, Levi, did not participate with the others in donating sacrifices for the inauguration of the Tabernacle. But G-d reassured him, "Yours is greater than theirs, for you will kindle and prepare the lights of the Menorah." Why should this task console Aharon, the Ramban asks, when in fact *all* the service done in the Tabernacle was entrusted to him?

The kindling of the Menorah was unique, explains Rav Chaim Shmulevitz. It took on a different quality than the other services. The purpose of the Menorah was to give the Jewish people the opportunity to thank G-d for the pillar of fire that lighted their way in the wilderness for forty years. This *mitzvah* was created "to raise you before the nations, who will say, 'Look how Israel is lighting for the One Who illuminates the entire world' " (*Bamidbar Rabbah* 15:5). Only the *mitzvah* of lighting the Menorah, as opposed to any of the other *mitzvos* associated with the Tabernacle, could be seen as *Klal Yisrael's* "repayment" to G-d for the goodness He had done for them. The Menorah symbolized their gratitude more than animal sacrifices.

My dear *chassan* and *kallah,* a key component in an everlasting marriage is the appreciation each partner feels for what the other is contributing to the relationship. By responding with this appreciation, each of you will gladly continue to nurture and provide for each other and your marriage. For your relationship to blossom, mutual appreciation is mandatory. May this lesson, among all the lessons of the Torah, be imbued in your hearts and your home.

Rabbi Dr. Moshe J. Yeres

פרשת יתרו
Parshas Yisro

THE *PARSHAH* OF *YISRO* contains the seminal event in Jewish history, the pronouncement of the Ten Commandments on Mount Sinai. These Commandments have special significance for a young couple not only because they enunciate the basic ideals of fidelity in a marriage — *"lo sinaf"* and *"lo sachmod"* — but because they mark the beginning of the Jewish people's mandate to be a holy nation. This event is reenacted on a smaller scale at every Jewish wedding through the *kiddushin* ceremony.

At a secular wedding ceremony, the bride and groom pledge themselves to each other with the words, "I do." Under the *chuppah, lehavdil*, there is also an "I do" in the hearts of the *chassan* and *kallah* — the "I do" of *"Naaseh venishma,"* the acceptance of G-d's will first pronounced by the Jewish people at Sinai: "We will do and we will listen" (*Shemos* 24:7). The *chassan* displays this commitment by placing the ring on his *kallah's* finger, consecrating her "according to the law of Moses and Israel." With these words, he declares that

---

Rabbi Yeres is rav of Congregation Ohav Zedek in Wilkes-Barre, Pennsylvania.

everything done under the *chuppah* is a perpetuation of Jewish law and fashions another link in the unbroken chain that reaches Sinai.

One's wedding day is a time of fresh beginnings, a day such as the one when the entire Jewish nation gathered at the base of Mount Sinai and declared for the first time, "*Naaseh venishma*." I do. We accept. The Jews, who had sunk to a level of nearly irredeemable spiritual debasement while in Egypt, were able to elevate themselves and return to G-d's good graces. With this one simple declaration, the Jews presented to G-d their commitment to start fresh and do all that He asks of them.

This commitment is also pledged by our *chassan* and *kallah*. On the day of their wedding, say our Sages, the sins of the young couple are forgiven. Marriage has that cleansing quality. It is a new beginning, a return to innocence and a commitment to the will of G-d through the founding of a new Jewish home.

Similarly, Moshe's father-in-law, Yisro, pursues a new beginning by entering the Israelites' camp. Why did he come? "*Vayishma Yisro*," the *pasuk* tells us. "And Yisro heard . . . all that G-d did for Moshe and His nation Israel" (18:1). What exactly did he hear that impelled him, at that point in his life, to join the Jewish nation?

The Talmud offers three opinions: "Rabbi Yehoshua says, 'He heard about the battle with Amaleik . . . .' Rabbi Eliezar Hamoda'i says, 'He heard about the giving of the Torah . . . .' Rabbi Elazar says, 'He heard about the splitting of the Red Sea' " (*Zevachim* 116a). Are we then to understand that Yisro's information was limited to just one of these events? No, explains the *Keli Yakar*, Yisro did hear of all three. The *tanna'im* in the Talmud merely disagree over which of the three impressed him to the point that he was prompted to leave his high position in Midyan and join his son-in-law's nation.

In a similar vein, there exist today different reasons for the modern Jew to be drawn to *Klal Yisrael*. Some people most identify with our faith when they perceive it as a source of strength and success. This was evident thirty years ago after Israel's victory in the Six-Day War, when many Jews renewed their commitment to Judaism, both religiously and materially. Just as Yisro was drawn to the Jews after hearing of G-d's might and His "outstretched arm" in splitting the Red Sea and vanquishing Pharaoh's chariots, many Jews identify with their people in times of triumph.

Others identify with their people at precisely the opposite times, when Jews are the victims, the underdogs, the scapegoats of a cruel society. For this reason the Holocaust remains a dominant component of modern Jewish identity. Yisro, too, identified with this nation of former slaves after hearing of Amaleik's dastardly attack upon them.

Lastly, there are those who identify with the Jewish people because they are the keepers of the Torah. An identification with *Klal Yisrael* based simply on victories or victimization will not endure — those are insufficient reasons for maintaining a commitment. Yisro also heard about Sinai. He heard of a people who received the Torah from G-d, and he, too, wanted to join in their mission.

This identification is necessary today as well. One can not be a solid Jew without accepting the *"Naaseh venishma"* of Sinai, without fully accepting the Torah and all that is in it. Our cultural, ethnic, historical and military ties contribute to our national profile, but they do not permanently bond us to our heritage. We require the bond of Torah and mitzvos to do that. Anything less is neither satisfying nor satisfactory.

My dear *chassan* and *kallah,* your life together will involve many experiences. Some will be moments of victory and happiness, which you will savor together and which will strengthen your love, your union and your home. Other times will be more difficult, challenging you to fight together against the modern Amaleiks that seek to weaken your convictions. Throughout both the triumphs and disappointments of life always remember, *"Vayishma."* Hear the voice of Torah, the voice of commitment to G-d's law, the voice of loyalty to His commandments. Then you will assure yourselves a strong Jewish home, one that will form the basis of your love and your bond, one that will enable you to further the legacy of the Jewish nation.

Rabbi Aaron Borow

פרשת יתרו
Parshas Yisro

HIS IS A HAPPY MOMENT FOR YOU and your families. May G-d bless you and your families with many occasions of *simcha*.

As you recently stood under the *chuppah,* may I remind you of the experience that the Jewish people had several thousand years ago. They also stood under a *chuppah* at Mount Sinai, when they became a people. G-d gave Israel the Torah while they stood at the foot of Sinai. G-d, as it were, was the *chassan* and the Jewish people, His *kallah.*

The *chuppah,* the canopy, is the symbol of Sinai and therefore should serve as a reminder of duties and responsibilities that you have to each other, to your parents and family, to our community and to our people in Israel.

Our sages tell us that the Almighty raised the mountain over the heads of the Israelites and it formed a *chuppah,* a canopy over them. G-d said to the Jewish people, "If you accept my laws, good; if not, here will be your grave." This is a perplexing Midrash. Israel had already expressed its willingness to accept the Torah! They made a commitment by saying *"Naaseh venishma."* Why was there a need for coercion?

Our sages answer that the Jewish people had accepted the *Torah Shebiksav*, the Written Law, which presented the broad principles of Judaism: Love your neighbor as yourself, remember the Shabbos and keep it holy, discipline your eating habits, live in accordance with the ethics of Judaism. The details of these duties, however, are not found in the Torah. How should one love a neighbor? How is the Shabbos to be observed? How does one keep kosher? How can one lead an ethical and moral life? These details were left to the *Torah Shebaal Peh*, to the Oral Law, to Jewish tradition. G-d said, your existence as Jews depends on your keeping not only the broad principles of Judaism, but also the little details.

Marriage has some large principles — it is based on love and mutual respect. You must always keep these broad principles in mind, but also you must not neglect the little details. A person who truly loves another thinks not only in terms of "I," but in terms of "we." In a healthy marriage, each partner is concerned about the happiness of the other. True love lasts because it includes these details — devotion, affection, sympathy, understanding, and enjoyment of common interests. True love endures when it includes G-d.

I believe that the fondest hopes of your parents and families will be for you to follow in the path of your forebears, to make the great principles of Judaism and also the little details an important part of your lives. These details, we believe, will enhance your lives and strengthen your marriage. May the prayers of your parents and loved ones for your happiness be fulfilled and may G-d bless you for many good years together.

Rabbi Howard Gershon

פרשת משפטים
Parshas Mishpatim

U PON BECOMING THE REBBE OF GER, the great sage known as the *Sefas Emes* made a startling announcement to his chassidim: During the recitation of Hallel on the upcoming holiday of Sukkos, any person who would say the verse in *Tehillim* that begins, "*Ana Hashem* — Please G-d...," with intense concentration and devotion would have all of his prayers answered.

It came as no surprise then that when Sukkos arrived, the chassidim came to the synagogue greatly anticipating the moment they would be able to say those words. They prayed breathlessly, their words of supplication reaching feverish proportions as the service arrived at Hallel. And when the congregation came to the verse, "Please G-d, save us; please G-d, make us successful" (*Tehillim* 118:25), the din in the great room was explosive. The delirious congregants shouted the words with great enthusiasm and conviction. After praying, the townspeople returned to their homes full of joy, convinced that all of their prayers would be fulfilled.

Rabbi Gershon is executive director of the Adolph Schreiber Hebrew Academy of Rockland in Monsey, New York.

After several months, seeing no noticeable transformations in their lives, the chassidim decided to send a delegation to the Rebbe to ask what had gone wrong. "We did as you said," they reminded him. "We cried out the verse, 'Please G-d, save us; please G-d, make us successful,' with great conviction, yet we don't see any changes."

The Rebbe smiled at them and said, "My dear children, you must have misunderstood me. I was not referring to that verse, but to a different verse found in Hallel — 'Please G-d, for I am Your servant' (116:16)."

It is this verse, wherein man declares his absolute devotion to G-d, that contains the ultimate human mission and that, when spoken with proper concentration, yields magnificent results.

The greatest status a Jew can achieve is to be a servant of G-d, and the importance of this idea is reflected in the first mitzvah of *Parshas Mishpatim*. The *pasuk* states that a Jew who is sold as a servant remains in his master's charge for six years, after which he may go free or, if he is content with his situation, he may remain a servant. The option to stay with his master, however, is not encouraged by the Torah, and he is, in fact, punished for this decision. The Torah demands that his ear be pierced.

Rashi, quoting the Midrash, explains the symbolism: This ear, which heard on Sinai "For to *Me* are the children of Israel servants" (*Vayikra* 25:55) and still went out and acquired another master for itself, should be pierced (*Shemos* 21:6). The Torah reminds us that we must always strive to be servants of G-d, not man. This is no easy task; even the greatest sages did not feel they had quite achieved that level of Divine service.

The Talmud (*Berachos* 34b) records the story of Rabbi Chanina ben Dosa and Rabbi Yochanan ben Zakkai, who studied Torah together. When the son of Rabbi Yochanan fell ill, he called upon his friend, Rabbi Chanina, to pray for him. The boy soon recovered and Rabbi Yochanan remarked to his wife that only Rabbi Chanina could have merited such Divine intervention. "Had I spent the entire day in prayer," he told her, "they [in the heavens] would not have listened to me." Even had he himself prayed all day for his own son, his prayers would not have been answered.

His wife did not understand why. "Is he greater than you?" she asked.

"No," replied Rabbi Yochanan. "But while I am only an officer of the

King, he is a servant of the King." Though they both dedicated their lives to serving the same G-d, their positions were different, in Rabbi Yochanan's view.

But one would think that an officer holds a higher rank in the King's court. Would not the words of an officer be taken more seriously than the words of a servant?

Rashi explains the distinction between the two. An officer can enter the king's chamber only when summoned, but a servant enters and leaves at will. He is at home in his master's palace. In this sense, he is superior to the officer.

Rashi offers another insight at the start of *Parshas Mishpatim*. What, he wonders, is the connection between this *parshah,* which comprises most of Jewish civil law, and the last verses in *Parshas Yisro*, which describe the construction of the altar in the Tabernacle? This is to teach us, Rashi explains, that the Sanhedrin, the Supreme Court, was to meet in the Holy Temple, in a room directly across from the altar.

The positioning is deliberate. One tends to think of *avodas Hashem*, Divine service, in terms of ritual-prayer, ceremonies, holidays. But often one neglects to associate his day-to-day schedule of activity with the notion of *avodas Hashem*. Perhaps this is why the Sanhedrin, which adjudicates the laws of *Parshas Mishpatim* — contracts, torts, property, the stuff of everyday life — was located next to the altar, the center of Divine service. This proximity served to remind those in the Temple, as it should remind us today, that all areas of life are covered by the Torah and find their place in the world of Torah. Hence, all areas of life contain opportunities for Divine service. By behaving properly, in accordance with Torah law in all matters of life, both holy and temporal, one accomplishes *avodas Hashem.*

My dear *chassan* and *kallah,* as you begin your life together, your goal should be to achieve the lofty level of *ovdei Hashem*, servants of G-d. You should feel at home in G-d's world, and by building a home of Torah and mitzvos, you will insure that G-d dwells in your midst. Through your efforts, you will merit the fulfillment of your hopes and dreams, as the Gerer Rebbe promised, and you will be blessed together with good health and happiness.

Rabbi A. Mark Levin

פרשת תרומה
Parshas Terumah

I.

THE CONSTRUCTION AND WORSHIP of the Golden Calf by the Jewish people almost brought about their destruction, which was averted only by Moshe Rabbeinu's strenuous intervention. Their violating the prohibition against idolatry, the second of the Ten Commandments, clearly deserved a capital response from G-d. In light of the severity of this prohibition, it seems odd that, in *Parshas Terumah*, G-d orders that two golden cherubim be set atop the Holy Ark, for, after the sin, why would G-d want a graven image, made from the same material as the calf was, to be prominently fixed upon the holiest object in the Tabernacle?

From this ironic twist one gains a vital insight: It is necessary at all times to distinguish between things that seem alike on the surface for in reality they are often antitheses. Opportunities in life that seem golden

Rabbi Levin is rav of Anshei Sphard-Beth El Emeth Congregation in Memphis, Tennessee.

will sometimes be as beneficial as the cherubim and at other times be as destructive as the Golden Calf. But how is one to know the difference?

The only way to know is to follow the word of G-d. Did G-d command the construction of the Golden Calf? No. Therefore its construction doomed the Jewish people. Did G-d command the fashioning of the cherubim? Yes. Therefore their manufacture was productive.

The need to choose carefully and correctly is especially important for a newlywed couple as they stand on the threshold of fashioning their own sanctuary, their home. A *chassan* and *kallah* must use discretion in determining which features of the society around them will be allowed to enter the sanctuary that is their home, and which elements will have to be kept out and extruded should they penetrate the walls of that sanctuary. To make these distinctions they must be sensitive to the word of G-d and this is where their Torah educations will serve them well.

These decisions become more critical when children are born to the family. The cherubim, say our Sages, had the faces of children. Nurturing the sensitive *neshamah* of a child requires the utmost prudence, and the mother and father must be prepared with a system for making a wide range of decisions.

II.

Immediately after describing the cherubim, G-d gives Moshe the measurements for the Shulchan, the special table that continually displayed twelve loaves of bread, which represented the twelve tribes of Israel. Every Shabbos, fresh loaves were baked to replace the old ones, which were then distributed to the *kohanim* — six to the shift that had served that week and six to the shift that was coming in. With only six loaves per shift to go around, the *kohanim* had to jockey for a bite of the bread. To a society where day-old bread is sold at half price and two-day-old bread not at all, this allowance of week-old bread does not seem like much of a delicacy. But this was no ordinary bread.

The Gemara asserts that "its removal was identical to its placement" (*Menachos* 29b). In other words, one week later the bread was as fresh as it had been the day it was baked. Through Divine intervention the bread retained its freshness. Herein lies another lesson offered by the *parshah* to a *chassan* and *kallah*. At their wedding, a couple is deeply in love with each other, passionately committed to each other. But over time, human nature is such that emotions, like bread, cool down and eventually become stale. This is the threat to every marriage — and the challenge.

Keeping a marriage fresh is only possible if the relationship contains Divine ingredients. Subjected to all sorts of influences — where they work and study, the people with whom they interact — the *chassan* and *kallah* are unlikely to remain the same people they were on the day of their wedding. Subsequently, these changes, however slight, impact upon their commitments. They therefore need to work on their relationship by learning together, experiencing together, sharing together. Even so, there are no guarantees of success. *Even so,* G-d's help is required. Only Jewish law and Jewish values, which have escorted the couple to the *chuppah,* can provide the guidelines, insights and means to renewing and replenishing their marriage.

III.

Every *chassan* and *kallah* enters a marriage with wonderful intentions for their relationship, the home and the life they will establish together. But are these intentions enough?

The answer to this question is supplied by the first verse of the *parshah.* G-d commands Moshe, "From every man whose heart propels him to give take My offering. This is the offering you shall take from them: gold, silver and copper" (*Shemos* 25:1-2).

There are two parts to this directive, Rabbi Akiva Eiger observes. First is intent. Only one "whose heart propels him to give" is solicited; participation is voluntary, an appeal to the generosity of the heart. Once idealism is determined, G-d brings His order down to its practical application: "gold, silver and copper." These are the materials needed to build the Tabernacle.

As far as G-d is concerned, the most important ingredient is the generosity of one's heart, one's openness. When it comes to building a Tabernacle, however, intentions alone are insufficient. To build, one needs physical materials. G-d is supremely interested in the intentions of his nation, but a Tabernacle can not be built with intentions alone.

The same holds true when building the sanctuary that is the Jewish home. If that home, that sanctuary, could be built solely by good intentions, by wonderful dreams alone, it would be the most splendid palace in the world. But intentions are not sufficient; those intentions need to be manifested in physical acts — the behavior of husband and wife toward each other, their sensitivity to each other's needs, their giving to each other selflessly and generously. The pooling of their talents, resources, energies and time along with their display of patience, understanding and forgiveness are what bring the noblest of intentions to fruition.

My dear *chassan* and *kallah,* you have proven yourselves to be masters of all the lessons of Parshas *Terumah.* Your ability to distinguish between the golden calves and the golden cherubim of this world, your dedication to Torah and mitzvos which is followed through with scrupulous observance, and your enthusiasm to learn and develop together will combine to insure that your marriage remains fresh and spirited and that your home will be consecrated as a residence of the L-rd.

Rabbi Yaakov Marcus

פרשת תצוה
Parshas Tetzaveh

THE FIRST STAGE OF THE MARRIAGE CEREMONY, known as *kiddushin*, occurs when the *chassan* places the ring on his beloved's finger while saying, "Behold, you are *mekudeshes* to me according to the law of Moshe and Israel." Although this declaration appears simple and straightforward, its composition is actually intricate.

The word *mekudeshes* means both designated and consecrated. In one sense, the *kallah* is designated as the wife of the *chassan*. But the choice of this word also indicates that marriage, rather than being a temporal union of man and woman, is in truth infused with sanctity. When someone is *mekadeish* an object, he consecrates it, setting it aside for G-d and apart from the rest of the world. By joining together in marriage, man and woman, too, set themselves apart from the rest of the world.

Kedushah denotes exclusivity. To be *mekadeish* is to separate in order to elevate. *Kedushah*, moreover, does not rest on the surface; it

Rabbi Marcus, editor of Genesis Jerusalem Press, is rav of the Young Israel of Staten Island, New York.

penetrates. For a Jewish marriage to be complete, sanctity must not merely be present but must be pervasive.

In order to understand this link between holiness and marriage, one must investigate the nature of both concepts as viewed by Jewish tradition.

Most informative is the section in *Parshas Tetzaveh* wherein G-d describes to Moshe the distinctive clothing the *kohanim* would wear when serving in the Temple. *Kohanim* have a special sanctity that has halachic ramifications to this day. But at the time of the Temple their holiness was even more apparent, especially while they performed the service.

At their head was the *kohein gadol,* representing the crown of the priesthood, who had a special wardrobe consisting of eight pieces of clothing, including an apron and a breastplate. The breastplate contained precious stones, which, when worn by the *kohein gadol,* rested upon his shoulders and heart. Etched into these gems were the names of the twelve tribes of Israel. Every time the *kohein gadol* entered the Tabernacle he was commanded to wear this uniform. Thus, when he performed the Divine service on behalf of the Jewish people, they were present upon his shoulders and his heart. Only when he carried on his shoulders the communal burden of the Jewish people, when his heart beat in unison with the national pulse, could the *kohein gadol* fulfill his sanctified mission.

This same commitment is required of partners in *kiddushin*. When two people marry they must strive to be one, to share one heartbeat, to share all burdens. Then they too are sanctified.

Another valuable lesson for the *chassan* and *kallah* is learned from the inclusion in the *kiddushin* formula of the phrase, "according to the law of Moshe and Israel." Why this phrase rather than simply, "according to the Torah"? Why does the *chassan's* declaration refer to the legacy of Moshe and the Jewish people?

The answer lies not in what is found in *Parshas Tetzaveh*, but in what is not found there. *Tetzaveh* is unique in that it is the only *parshah*, after his birth, not to mention Moshe's name. This omission came from Moshe's persistence that G-d forgive the Jews for worshiping the Golden Calf, "and if not, please erase me from Your book that You wrote" (*Shemos* 32:32). Although G-d ultimately did forgive His people,

Moshe's request was still heeded to a limited extent. The Gemara (*Berachos* 32a) states that Moshe was risking his life for the Jewish people when he issued this ultimatum.

Moshe's relationship with the Jewish people was one of absolute devotion and self-sacrifice, and is therefore inserted into the *kiddushin* formula. When a man and a woman are married they become bound to one another in selfless devotion just as Moshe was bound to the Jewish people. The process of *kiddushin* is marked by unqualified altruism.

Marriage in Jewish terms, therefore, involves unity, responsibility and sacrifice. Exactly how are these qualities infused into a relationship? Again, *Parshas Tetzaveh* provides an answer.

The description of the priests' clothing and their inauguration into G-d's service is sandwiched between the command to light the Menorah and the commands to bring the daily animal sacrifices and incense offering. It seems that the planning of the inaugural ceremony is out of place in the middle of three commands regarding daily services. Why are these sections grouped together? Is there a connection between them?

Yes. The common denominator of all three services is their description as "*tamid,*" constant. The Menorah, which was lit every night, is described as "*ner tamid*" (*Shemos* 27:20), the twice-daily sacrifice is called "*olas tamid*" (29:42), and the incense offered every morning is termed "*ketores tamid*" (30:8). By surrounding the consecration of the priesthood with descriptions of these three services, the Torah sends a powerful message: The only way to remain dedicated to G-d is through constant service. A burning desire to fulfill the A-mighty's will is essential but not sufficient. Such passion must be concretized, supported by unrelenting action.

My dear *chassan* and *kallah,* the overwhelming feelings of love and devotion that engulf you as a newlywed couple are lofty, beautiful and, yes, holy. But they are just a beginning. Emotions ebb and flow like the raging waves of a stormy sea. The most intense yearning of a human being can fade as swiftly as a fleeting cloud. Only when those feelings are buttressed by ceaseless demonstrations of commitment are they crystalized. Only then can a successful Jewish home be built. With sacrifice and responsibility demonstrated mutually and constantly you will bring *kedushah* to your *kiddushin* and merit the realization of your dreams together as you build a home infused with sanctity.

Rabbi Harry Levinson

פרשת כי תשא
Parshas Ki Sisa

ARSHAS KI SISA BEGINS WITH G-d commanding Moshe, *"Ki sisa es rosh benei Yisrael* — When you take a census of the Israelites to determine their numbers, each one shall be counted by giving an atonement offering for his life" (*The Living Torah*, *Shemos* 30:12). The idea that G-d counts the Jewish people is a sublime one, marked in the literal translation of the words *ki sisa*, which mean, "when you raise." When G-d counts the Jewish people He elevates them; He proves them worthy of being counted.

Shlomo Hamelech celebrates this idea in *Shir Hashirim* (7:3), describing the beauty of the Jewish nation in metaphor: "*Bitneich areimas chitim, sugah bashoshanim*," literally, "Your belly is a heap of grain, enclosed by roses."

"Why is Israel analogized to grain?" asks the Midrash. "Reish Lakish says, Just as this grain is measured, so too all Israel was counted" (*Yalkut Shimoni*).

The *Keli Yakar* elaborates. Objects such as straw, which are not special, are not counted, but objects such as grain are counted and

---

Rabbi Levinson is an attorney from Monsey, New York.

measured. The Jews are like grain — every one is counted and measured; every Jew has significance.

Moreover, the Jews are distinguished from the rest of the world not only on an intellectual and moral level. Even on a physical level, where one would think that the Jew and the Gentile are on equal footing, as both have identical physical needs, the Jew is on an elevated level. Shlomo Hamelech underscores the Jews physicality because a Jew distinguishes himself through his material comportment as well. By following the Torah's mandates, the Jew infuses the physical aspects of his world with holiness.

The need to sanctify one's material living is a critical one for every married couple. How do they bring this holiness into their home? By following the example of the Tabernacle's construction.

G-d calls upon Betzalel to construct the utensils for the Tabernacle. The Gemara (*Berachos* 55a) records that Moshe told Betzalel to build "the Ark, utensils and the Tabernacle," to which Betzalel responded, "Our teacher Moshe, the custom of the world is that a man [first] builds a house and afterwards brings his possessions into it. Yet you are telling me to build the Ark [first, and then] the utensils and the Tabernacle. Where shall I put the utensils that I build? Perhaps G-d said to you, '[First build the] Tabernacle, [then the] Ark and utensils.' "

Moshe acknowledged that Betzalel was correct. First the Tabernacle needed to be built and then its furnishings.

Every married couple sets out to build the perfect Jewish home, and the way for them to accomplish this goal is outlined in this *parshah*.

First, *chassan* and *kallah* must see themselves the way the Torah sees them, as worthy members of a holy nation. *"Ki sisa es rosh benei Yisrael."* They must show respect and deference to each other as well as to every member of the Jewish people. Then they will fully appreciate the responsibility and honor placed upon them as members of G-d's chosen nation.

Second, they must actively pursue that responsibility. Their commitment to Torah values can not be limited to the realm of good intentions. Torah can not be restricted to the mind, to the intellect, to a "higher consciousness," but must also extend to actions in the material world. In that way, your physical and material attributes will also be elevated, *"sugah bashoshanim,"* enclosed by the sweet scent of the *mitzvos* that you do. The mundane activities of your everyday lives will ascend to higher, spiritual levels along with your regular observance of the *mitzvos.*

Third, you must aspire to be like Betzalel, who, as his name signified, lived "*betzeil Keil* — in the shadow of G-d." You must build your home to resemble the Tabernacle, to be a mini-sanctuary, a home where service of G-d and observance of His Torah are the first concern. Once you build that structure, you will have room for the "utensils," the blessings of prosperity that will be yours.

My dear *chassan* and *kallah,* may you build a sanctified home with the building blocks of personal prestige, passionate commitment to the Torah, faithful observance of the *mitzvos,* and the infusion of Torah into every aspect of your life together. By following these steps, your home will be blessed and will radiate light and warmth to all around you. It will be a sanctuary for all to see and for all to be inspired by.

Professor Shimon Kwestel

פרשת ויקהל
Parshas Vayakheil

E

VERYONE WHO ATTENDS A WEDDING expresses their wish to the newlyweds that they will build a *bayis ne'eman beYisrael* — a faithful Jewish home. Their wishes are a beautiful blessing to the *chassan* and *kallah,* yet it remains the young couple's responsibility to do what is necessary to transform that noble sentiment into reality. While this is no easy task, G-d has illuminated the way toward its fulfillment.

In *Parshas Vayakheil*, Moshe instructs Betzalel to make the Holy Ark, with two cherubim standing atop, "their faces turned toward each other," spreading their wings over the ark (*Shemos* 37:9).

In *Divrei Hayamim*, however, the verse describing the dimensions of the cherubim that Shlomo Hamelech placed in the Holy Temple states that "their faces were toward the house" (II:3:13). According to Radak, the cherubim faced east, toward the sanctuary, meaning that they stood side by side and were not facing each other. According to his opinion, why were the cherubim in the Temple positioned differently from those in the Tabernacle?

Professor Kwestel, past president of the Orthodox Union, is a professor at Touro Law School.

The Gemara (*Bava Basra* 99a) explains that the cherubim in the Temple were constructed just as Moshe described them, facing each other. But they remained facing each other only as long as the Jewish people followed G-d's commands. When, during the reign of Shlomo Hamelech, the Jewish people failed to follow G-d's will, the cherubim turned away from each other and stood side by side, facing the sanctuary. Only when we follow His commands and subordinate our wishes and desires to those of G-d will the cherubim face each other.

To create an everlasting home, the *chassan* and *kallah* must be like the cherubim and face each other. They both must be sensitive to the wishes and desires of their partner and be prepared to subordinate their own desires to those of their spouse, just as they both must subordinate their desires to G-d's commandments. If they are successful in this mutual sacrifice, they will achieve a balance that will enable them to grow together.

The ability of the *chassan* and *kallah* to face each other is similarly an essential ingredient in building and maintaining the sanctuary that is the Jewish home. This can be achieved by being a *nediv leiv* — by giving of oneself voluntarily and wholeheartedly. This quality was demonstrated in the wilderness by the entire Jewish nation when it came time for the actual construction of the Tabernacle. G-d commanded Moshe to collect from the Jewish people the gold, silver, copper, skins, stones, wood and wool needed for the project. Yet G-d never specified how much to give. That decision was left to each Jew. Immediately, "the entire community of the children of Israel departed from before Moshe" (*Shemos* 35:20) to go to their homes and bring their contributions. They were not just willing but eager to supply with a full heart what was necessary — without looking at what the other was doing.

My dear *chassan* and *kallah,* what is the secret to building a sanctuary for a home? Each of you must not simply provide for the other but you must do so freely, anxiously and wholeheartedly, without expecting anything in return, motivated solely by the desire to make each other happy. You must keep your home focused on spiritual development, continually learning and growing. If you are successful in bringing these ingredients into your marriage, you will create an unbreakable bond and a home in which the cherubim see eye to eye and reflect the sanctity that G-d bestows upon every good union.

Michael J. Muschel, M.D.

פרשת פקודי
Parshas Pekudei

ARSHAS PEKUDEI CHRONICLES THE FINAL PHASES in the construction and preparation of the Tabernacle, culminating
with its assembly on Rosh Chodesh Nissan. The lessons of
this *parshah* serve as a blueprint for a *chassan* and *kallah* as they embark
on a similar journey — for Biblical and Midrashic literature view a
Jewish household as a Tabernacle of one's own, a miniature of the
sanctuary that the Jews built in the wilderness.

A cursory review of the *parshah* reveals an oddity. The Torah states at
the start of the *parshah* that Betzalel "did everything that the L-rd had
commanded Moshe" (*Shemos* 38:22). A few verses later, the Torah
states that he made "the holy garments that were for Aharon, as the L-rd
had commanded Moshe" (39:1). Next the Torah describes each piece of
clothing that was tailored for the priesthood, stating at the conclusion of
each that it was made to specification, "as the L-rd had commanded
Moshe." The Torah concludes this chapter with the declaration that
"The children of Israel did all of the work just as the L-rd had
commanded Moshe" (39:42).

Dr. Muschel is a practicing cardiologist in Monsey, New York.

This phrase continues to appear in the next chapter as Moshe erected the Tabernacle and placed all of its utensils inside. He brought in the Holy Ark "as the L-rd had commanded Moshe" (40:21); he set the shewbread on its special table "as the L-rd had commanded Moshe" (40:23); he lit the lamps of the Menorah "as the L-rd had commanded Moshe" (40:25). And so on throughout the chapter.

The Torah obviously goes to great lengths to impress upon its reader that every movement in the construction of the Tabernacle was done "as the L-rd had commanded Moshe." Would anyone have thought otherwise? Why the need to spell this out over and over? Why such prolixity?

The *Beis Haleivi* justifies this tedious redundancy with reference to a Midrash, which defines the purpose of the Tabernacle as expiation for the Jews' sin of worshiping the Golden Calf. The people of Israel, he points out, were well intentioned in building the Golden Calf; their goal was to continue some form of Divine service while Moshe tarried in the skies. Their tragic flaw, however, was in thinking they could appeal to their own judgement, to reason and arrive at an appropriate means of religious worship. They failed to recognize that a common sense approach to religous service is insufficient. Only a mandate from G-d, only a Divine imperative, can render a particular ritual meaningful and worthy.

The construction of the Tabernacle was a catharsis for the disappointment of this error. In building the Tabernacle, the Jewish people reapplied their means toward worshipping G-d purely, in a manner mandated by Him, rather than in a way they saw fit. Thus, every detail, no matter how obvious or logical, was contingent upon G-d's approval and every step was executed only after careful determination that this was the exact way it was to be done "as the L-rd had commanded Moshe." The repetition of this phrase throughout the *parshah* emphasizes the Jews complete submission to G-d's will and their unwillingness to rely on their own human judgement.

This concept extends to the sanctuary that is the Jewish home. A Jewish home requires vigilance in holding G-d's word — as opposed to personal conclusions — paramount. One could argue that the ceremony of *chuppah* and *kiddushin* is nothing more than a restyling of civil marriage, an institution warranted by simple common sense, establishing a matrix for family and a framework for social interaction. In this view, marriage is a time-honored tradition, a sensible product of human social theory, bereft of any spiritual significance.

But the Jewish view of marriage is of a union sanctified by the Torah's instruction, endowed with the holiness of halachic behavior. This transcendental quality of the Jewish marital bond is beautifully captured in a conversation between Moshe and Betzalel. Moshe commanded Betzalel first to construct the utensils of the Tabernacle and then to build its actual structure. But this order struck Betzalel as not quite right. "The custom of the world," he submitted, "is to first build the house and then to furnish it." Moshe agreed. "You have been standing in the shadow of G-d (*betzeil Keil*), for that is certainly how G-d commanded me" (Rashi, *Shemos* 38:22), and so Betzalel first constructed the Tabernacle and then its furnishings.

Betzalel's comment is as pertinent today as it was in the wilderness. Contemporary society has produced couples who, after their engagement, concern themselves right away with rings and clothes, with appliances and china. Betzalel gives the proper sequence. First the foundation of the home must be established, distinguished as a sanctuary, modeled after the precepts of the Torah. Once that is accomplished, the furnishings can be put in place, and then those furnishings, having been introduced into such an environment, will become elevated to the status of holy objects.

Everything that finds itself within the walls of such a home finds itself within the four walls of *halachah* and is transformed, for everything in that home is focused on Divine service. Under the roof of a sanctuary, all things — from material objects to children — are elevated by this direction. The family that exists in such a home eats, drinks, dresses and lives under the aura of a Torah lifestyle. In this manner, one's daily, mundane concerns are raised to the exalted title of sacred service.

The centrality of this concept is evidenced by the declaration made under the *chuppah*. The *chassan* slips his ring onto the *kallah's* finger while declaring their relationship consecrated "according to the law of Moshe and Israel." On one level, these words are affirming this ritual as a binding contract, conforming to rigorous halachic standards. On a deeper level, though, both parties are acknowledging their entrance into a relationship that is infinitely more sublime by virtue of the imprint of "the law of Moshe and Israel." The Torah way of life will educate and sanctify this marriage from its very inception.

The same idea finds expression in the sixth of the *sheva berachos*, which asks G-d to "gladden the beloved friends as You gladdened Your creation in the Garden of Eden of old. Blessed are You, L-rd, Who gladdens the *chassan* and the *kallah.*" Initially, the two are referred to as beloved friends and their relationship is compared to that of Adam and Chavah in Eden, a utopian existence perhaps, but one that preceded the receiving of the Torah. The blessing ends, though, with reference to a relationship imbued with the sanctity of Torah, one that is lifted to a higher sphere, a place where man and woman can claim their crowns as *chassan* and *kallah.*

My dear *chassan* and *kallah,* it is not often that one encounters a young couple who so clearly grasp the deep religious significance of the bond they are just beginning to forge; a couple who leave us with no doubt that their every endeavor together shall be "according to the law of Moshe and Israel"; a couple who will build their home with the same principle that guided the construction of the Tabernacle, "as the L-rd had commanded Moshe"; a couple who are products of homes where Betzalel's footsteps are still heard, who learned firsthand that every mundane act within a household can be elevated to the status of sanctified service. When we behold such a couple as you, who are more than beloved friends, who have achieved the loftier level of *chassan* and *kallah,* we rejoice and wish you only blessings.

Sefer Vayikra

Dr. Paul Ratzker

פרשת ויקרא
Parshas Vayikra

THE *TANNA* IN *AVOS* (5:26) INSTRUCTS US to delve deeply into the Torah, for the Torah contains the essence of life. One must keep this sage advice in mind when searching through the *parshah* of *Vayikra* for an appropriate message for a *chassan* and *kallah*. The parshah deals exclusively with the animal sacrifices brought in the Tabernacle and later in the Temple, and on the surface has no practical application to a newlywed couple.

The *parshah* begins, "And [G-d] called to Moshe, and the L-rd spoke to him from the sanctuary" (*Vayikra* 1:1). Many commentators are intrigued by the phrasing of this initial verse: What does it mean that G-d first *called* to Moshe and then spoke to him? What is the significance of this sequence?

Rashi explains that before speaking with Moshe or issuing him any commands, G-d would first call for him — as a means of introduction. "*Vayikra*," says Rashi, "is a term of affection, a term used by the

---

Dr. Ratzker is chief neurosurgical resident at Jackson Memorial Hospital in Miami, Florida.

heavenly angels." This term is contrasted with the one used at the start of G-d's conversation with the evil prophet Bilam, the phonetically similar "*Vayikar* — And [G-d] appeared. . ." (*Bamidbar* 23:4), suddenly, without warning. But in His love for Moshe, G-d would preface every message to him with an introduction.

The Gemara does not relinquish this courtesy to the sphere of Biblical commentary, but instead applies G-d's example to everyone. "Why did calling precede speaking?" the Gemara asks. "The Torah taught proper manners. A person should not say something to his friend unless he calls him first" (*Yoma* 4b). In other words, one should not initiate conversation suddenly.

The same point is made in *Masechas Derech Eretz* (5): "Every person should learn proper manners from the Omnipresent, Who stood at the entrance to the Garden [of Eden] and called to Adam, as it says, 'And the L-rd called to Adam and said to him. . .' (*Bereishis* 3:9)."

Once again, one sees how G-d deals with those whom He cherishes. Yet, the *Torah Temimah* wonders why the Gemara bases its lesson on a verse from *Vayikra* when it could have chosen the earlier verse from *Bereishis*, the very one quoted in *Derech Eretz*, to teach the same lesson. Why choose a different verse?

The *Torah Temimah* offers a brilliant distinction. Rather than repeat the lesson first learned through G-d's treatment of Adam and noted in *Derech Eretz*, the Gemara wishes to broaden it. For G-d's relationship with Adam was not similar to His relationship with Moshe. Though G-d spoke to Adam many times, He had a more intimate relationship with Moshe, who, the Torah tells us, was the only person to speak with G-d "face to face."

The Gemara specifically chose the verse in *Vayikra*, where G-d called to Moshe, to teach that even when one wishes to talk to someone with whom he is very familiar, with whom he is in daily contact, with whom he maintains a comfortable, affectionate relationship, it is still improper to abruptly begin a conversation. "In my entire house he is trusted," G-d said of Moshe, and still, G-d formally addressed him before every discussion.

This lesson in *derech eretz* is one of the foundations of interpersonal relationships and especially crucial for married couples. What two people have a closer, more loving relationship than husband and wife?

Still, the Torah sets protocol, instructing that consideration must prevail.

The specific lesson of the need for a proper introduction is a mere representation of the sweeping, salient message of *derech eretz.* Proper behavior between people, no matter how comfortable they are with each other, is mandatory. *Derech eretz* must pervade even our most intimate lives. Close contact and communication do not negate respect and proper behavior. On the contrary, demonstrations of respect only increase a couple's affection for each other and set the tone for the comportment of the entire household. The way parents behave toward each other has, quite naturally, a profound effect on the attitude and behavior of their children.

Children who grow up in homes where *derech eretz* is practiced and promoted will display those traits among their friends, creating a positive influence that will contribute to the entire Jewish nation.

My dear *chassan* and *kallah,* by underscoring the feelings of affection and intimacy which you surely share at this moment with the qualities of respect and honor, you capitalize on the mark of an extraordinary relationship. Coming from families whose *derech eretz* is ingrained, you are both acutely aware of the importance of even the most subtle gesture. Along with kindness and compassion, selflessness and sensitivity, we are confident you will imbue your family with *derech eretz* and build a Jewish home worthy of our respect, admiration and blessing.

Rabbi Jeffrey Bienenfeld

פרשת צו

Parshas Tzav

OUR SAGES OFFER A MENU of observations, blessings, maxims and advice with regard to marriage. Many of them are beautifully straightforward, some are subtle, and others seem cryptic, in need of closer examination.

The Talmud, for example, minces no words in describing the marvel of two people finding each other: "It is as difficult to pair [two people in marriage] as splitting the Red Sea" (*Sotah* 2a). What is so difficult about finding one's life partner so as to warrant this comparison? Is meeting one's mate so miraculous an event?

Another statement of the Talmud which is puzzling at first glance is the assertion that one who rejoices before the *chassan* at his wedding is considered to have brought a thanksgiving offering (*Berachos* 6b). What does the Talmud mean to say by drawing this analogy? Where is the common ground upon which a wedding celebration and a thanksgiving offering both rest?

Rabbi Bienenfeld is rav of the Young Israel of St. Louis, Missouri.

In order to understand the Talmud's intent one must look at the components of a thanksgiving offering, which are described in *Parshas Tzav*. The thanksgiving offering was paradoxical in its composition. It was the only offering in the Temple to require both *chameitz* and matzah. What lies behind this mysterious merger?

The Torah sees a religious expression of thanks in this mixture of two diametrical ingredients because they symbolize the union of man and G-d. Man — finite, imperfect, mortal — is given the opportunity to attach himself to G-d — infinite, omnipotent, eternal. The A-mighty watches over His servants. He reaches out and rescues them from the earthiness of this world, allowing them to obtain spirituality when they cling to Him. G-d establishes a rendezvous in the Temple for His servants to reach Him. For this alone, man owes the A-mighty much thanks.

And how better to symbolize that gratitude than via a sacrifice that reconciles the polar concepts of *chameitz* and matzah. In fact, the thanksgiving offering teaches that all elements of the world, despite their heterogeneity, belong to G-d alone and find reconciliation through Him. Our Sages have even declared that in Messianic times all sacrifices will terminate save this unusual thanksgiving offering.

As with G-d and man, when turning to marriage, one sees an analogous incompatibility. Like *chameitz* and matzah, men and women are dissimilar, even opposites in many respects. They are different in their thinking patterns and emotional repertoire. They relate to others and they react to circumstances in distinct ways. With the gulf that separates the genders, is it conceivable that a man and a woman can join their lives together without constant conflict?

The Talmud emphatically responds in the affirmative. Just as *chameitz* and matzah converge to form an offering to G-d, so too can man and woman merge their distinct natures to become husband and wife — so long as G-d remains the constant focus of their relationship. When a Jewish family begins, with Jewish values and concerns at its core, happiness is sure to follow, and such a family will have much to be thankful for.

Likewise, those family and friends who come together to celebrate a Jewish marriage, who come to witness and rejoice over the merging of two distinct members of *Klal Yisrael* into one, are considered to have brought a thanksgiving offering in the Temple. They honor two wonderful people who, for all their differences, have boldly and lovingly chosen to bridge the human chasm with their devotion to a single, uncompromising conviction: G-d's Torah and *mitzvos* are the bedrock of a meaningful, spiritual life. With this conviction, their lives will blend together and forge a foundation upon which they can build "a faithful house in the community of Israel."

My dear *chassan* and *kallah,* all of those present today have come together to bring a symbolic thanksgiving offering. Our presence affirms the belief that each of you possesses a unique Divine imprint — that, as with any two people, you have different talents, different ways of thinking, different reactions to circumstances. Yet, with all of your differences, you are still capable of coming together, merging yourselves into a single unit.

What links you and serves as the foundation of your union is your single-minded devotion to G-d, His Torah and His *mitzvos,* and your inflexible belief in the Jewish mission. Upon this ironclad belief there is much common ground, ground upon which to build a fruitful home blessed with the sanctity of G-d and Israel. Our wish for you is that you continue to blend and grow together in the image of G-d and, amid the chaos of this world, establish your family upon the solid ground that is the inheritance of *Klal Yisrael.*

Rabbi Nosson Fromowitz

פרשת שמיני

פרשת שמיני
Parshas Shemini

FEW MOMENTS IN LIFE COMPARE to the one enjoyed at the time of matrimony. Marriage is a true Jewish *simcha* celebrated with seven blessings for the new couple.

The fifth of these *sheva berachos* asks G-d to gladden the *chassan* and *kallah* "as You gladdened Your creations in the Garden of Eden." The happiness of Adam and Chavah is singled out as the supreme example of the blessing one wishes upon every Jewish union. Why did our Sages choose their relationship as the standard for this blessing?

Soon after his creation, the Torah informs us, Adam became lonely. G-d brought before him all the creatures of the earth from which he could choose a mate, but Adam found none suitable. So G-d fashioned for him a mate from one of Adam's own sides; G-d created Chavah from within.

This sequence was no accident. G-d had a strategy. His intention was for Adam to experience a period of loneliness and yearning in order to

---

Rabbi Fromowitz is executive director of the Yeshiva of Spring Valley, in Monsey, New York.

intensify the love and appreciation he would feel once his life's partner was created. Owing to this series of events, Adam and Chavah knew that they were, literally, made for each other.

The happiness that accompanies the knowledge of having found one's true soul-mate is the happiness we wish for every new couple in the *sheva berachos* blessing.

The nature of this happiness is further reflected in a distinction between the fifth and sixth blessings. The fifth blesses G-d "Who gladdens the *chassan* and *kallah,*" whereas the sixth blesses G-d "Who gladdens the *chassan with* the *kallah.*" The distinction is subtle but powerful.

First, we wish each of them, the *chassan* and the *kallah,* a personal joy. We recognize them as two individual people, each with a unique background and education, each striving for self-perfection, each requiring and deserving a separate blessing, one that fits his or her original mission.

Next, we bless them together, as a single entity — *chassan with kallah.* We wish them happiness and success as a family unit, as another stone in the grand structure of *Am Yisrael.* With this blessing we emphasize that the individual accomplishments of each were but a prelude for all that is to come in their lifetime together.

For all our good intentions, one must still ask: How can a couple live up to these blessings of happiness? An important ingredient for marital success can be gleaned from the description in *Parshas Shemini* of the Tabernacle's inauguration.

After the Tabernacle is erected, the Torah details Aharon's every move as he performs the service for the first time. He slaughters and skins and readies the animals for the altar. But, according to the text, just before G-d sends down a fire from Above to consume the meat, Moshe and Aharon convene in an adjacent tent. No explanation is given for the sudden interruption of the day's main event. What was so important that it had to be discussed at the very moment the Jewish people were all assembled, anticipating the culmination of Aharon's inaugural service? What was the purpose of this sideline conference?

Rashi fills in the missing scenes. Though one would not be aware of it from reading the text, the fire that descended from the heavens almost didn't. Aharon and Moshe waited for G-d to send down His fire to consume the offerings, but it did not come. Aharon blamed himself. "I know that G-d is angry with me," he said. "And because of me, His Presence did not descend upon Israel" (*Vayikra* 9:23). Moshe then accompanied him to the tent where they both prayed and sought G-d's mercy.

How atypical and honorable was Aharon's response to a terribly embarrassing situation. Aharon certainly could have looked elsewhere for a legitimate reason for this failure. His actions that day were not a personal effort. In attempting to prevail upon G-d to rest His Divine Presence among the Jewish people, Aharon was not representing himself, but the entire nation of Israel. He could have faulted the nation for not being worthy. Why should he accept liability for G-d's reluctance? Why should he blame himself when others' shortcomings could have been responsible?

But he does. Aharon's reaction demonstrates his selflessness, the dedication he felt toward his nation to the extent that he publicly took personal responsibility when events went awry. He did not look beyond his own shortcomings to explain what had happened.

My dear *chassan* and *kallah,* though you are now married, you remain two individual people, with unique needs and capabilities. Each of you is deserving of a distinct *berachah*. By joining your futures together and embarking on the journey of life, you also receive a joint *berachah*, one that wishes you happiness together as a couple. To earn the rewards of this *berachah* and achieve the happiness contained in it, you must turn to the model of Aharon and Moshe: Aharon, who shouldered the burden of blame when failure confronted him, and Moshe, who assisted him in correcting that failure, joining him under one roof, praying with him. Together they were successful in winning G-d's favor.

This *simcha* marks the inauguration of your personal Tabernacle. Together the two of you enter your own tent — the home you are just starting to build, a home built on a foundation of Torah and love of G-d. By working together to overcome life's obstacles and rise to meet its challenges, you will grow and prosper, attaining the *berachah* of happiness as individuals, happiness as a family and insuring that the Divine Presence rests upon your home.

Rabbi Benjamin Yudin

פרשת תזריע־מצורע
Parshas Tazria-Metzora

HOUGH THE TWO *PARSHIOS* OF *Tazria* and *Metzora* deal exclusively with matters of spiritual impurity and it would therefore seem difficult to find within them an appropriate message for a *chassan* and *kallah*, there is a powerful insight present.

The Ramban writes that the affliction of *tzaraas* has no place in the natural order of the world, but is strictly a spiritual disease, meted out to Jews who do not follow G-d's precepts (*Vayikra* 13:47). Conversely, Jews who do maintain an appropriate level of observance ensure that their bodies, their clothes and their homes are granted a special Divine aura. For this reason, the Ramban continues, *tzaraas* was only inflicted in Eretz Yisrael, G-d's chosen land and residence, where the spiritual stakes are higher.

The spiritual connection between G-d and His nation is often compared to that of a *chassan* and *kallah*. Rashi notes that the verse, "On the day Moshe finished (*kalos*) erecting the Tabernacle ..."

Rabbi Yudin is rav of Congregation Shomrei Torah of Fair Lawn, New Jersey.

(*Bamidbar* 7:1), alludes to Israel's designation, on the day G-d's residence was established, as a *kallah* entering the *chuppah*.

The last mishnah in *Taanis* makes a similar connection. Quoting the verse, "Go out and see, daughters of Zion, King Shlomoh with the crown that his mother crowned him with on the day of his wedding and on the day his heart was glad" (*Shir Hashirim* 3:11), the mishnah states that "the day of his wedding" refers to the anniversary of the giving of the Torah.

Moreover, the *chuppah* canopy is symbolic of the mountain that G-d hung over the heads of the Jewish people when He gave them the Torah. Under that *chuppah* we break a glass to signify the destruction of the Temple and our subsequent estrangement from G-d. In all these instances there is a connection between a Jewish wedding and the Jews' marriage to G-d and His Torah, and both *Parshas Tazria* and *Metzora* contain laws that contribute to this correlation.

The end of *Parshas Metzora* establishes the laws of family purity, which govern the virtue of the Jewish people. In the *Zohar*, Rabbi Shimon bar Yochai teaches that by getting married, one complies with the verse, "Man shall leave his father and his mother and cling (*vedavak*) to his wife" (*Bereishis* 2:24), thus learning how to achieve the highest level of spirituality, *deveikus*, attachment to G-d. By bonding with his wife, a man develops his emotional capacity, which he can then apply to his relationship with G-d. Through marriage one comes closer to G-d.

More lessons in spiritual progress are gleaned from the beginning of *Parshas Tazria*. The *parshah* opens by declaring that the circumcision of a newborn son be on the eighth day. Rabbi Shimon bar Yochai suggests that the eighth day was chosen because, in accordance with Biblical law, after a weeklong period of abstinence following the birth of their child, the parents were permitted to resume marital relations on that day (*Nidah* 31b). As such, the *mitzvah* of *milah* is fulfilled at a time when the parents are especially happy, reflecting an ideal harmony between body and soul.

After the child is circumcised he is blessed that he should graduate "to Torah, to *chuppah* and to good deeds." The sequence of this blessing is revealing. Although the boy will likely perform acts of kindness prior to getting married, *chuppah* is mentioned first. Why?

Because the good deeds one accomplishes after proceeding to the *chuppah* are of a higher caliber, enhanced by a new lifestyle, intensified by a newfound capacity to care and share. Marriage promotes one's relationship with G-d and with fellow human beings. Marriage is enriching to both body and soul.

Moreover, these two *mitzvos,* family purity and circumcision, are identified with two distinct expressions of happiness. The Talmud states that the verse, "I rejoice (*sas*) in Your word" (*Tehillim* 119:162), refers to the commandment of *milah* (*Shabbos* 130a). And when exempting a newlywed from army duty, the Torah instead commands him "to make his wife glad (*vesimach*)" (*Devarim* 24:5). These two expressions of happiness — *sason* and *simcha* — are also found in the last of the seven blessings, when we thank G-d, "Who created *sason* and *simcha*, *chassan* and *kallah.*"

Though these two words appear to be the same, the Vilna Gaon insists there is a distinction. *Sason*, the Gaon explains, is happiness that occurs when reflecting on the past, happiness that follows accomplishment. *Simcha*, on the other hand, occurs when looking toward the future, happiness that emanates from the anticipation of things to come.

The words of the Shabbos prayer, "*Keil Adon*," reflect this distinction. The poem describes the angels as "*semeichim betzeisam vesasim bevo'am*" — when they leave on their missions they are *semeichim*; but upon return they are *sasim*. Before their mission they are hopeful, afterward they are grateful.

My dear *chassan* and *kallah,* under the *chuppah* we also employ these two locutions: *sason* for the past, for the joy in the two of you finding each other, for everything that has led to and contributed to this moment; and *simcha* for the future, for the happy, productive life we are sure you will make together, and for the Torah home you will build to be a source of pride and inspiration for your families and community.

Dr. David Luchins

פרשת אחרי מות
Parshas Acharei Mos

THE DRAMA AND MAJESTY of the Yom Kippur service in the Tabernacle and in the Temple is the leitmotif of *Parshas Acharei Mos*. The similarities between the service of Yom Kippur and the marriage ceremony have been noted by our Sages: Simple white garments, worn by the *kohein gadol* on Yom Kippur in Temple times, are today worn by both *chassan* and *kallah* under the *chuppah*. Customarily, *chassan* and *kallah* do not see each other for the seven days leading up to their wedding, just as the *kohein gadol* was sequestered for the week prior to Yom Kippur. And one's wedding day, like Yom Kippur, is a day of atonement for past misdeeds. These similarities demonstrate a pattern inviting speculation as to the role of marriage in Jewish tradition and the nature of a Jewish celebration.

There is a *mitzvah* to be *mesamei'ach* the *chassan,* to make him happy, and one accomplishes this, says the Gemara, by praising the qualities of the *kallah* (*Kesubos* 16b). Curiously though, there is no

---

Dr. Luchins is chairman of the political science department at Touro College and senior assistant to United States Senator Daniel Patrick Moynihan.

corresponding *mitzvah* that specifically requires one to be *mesamei'ach* the *kallah,* nor is there any mention of singing the *chassan's* praises. In order to understand this discrepancy one must understand the nature of *simcha*.

Rav Eliyahu Meir Bloch, the Telzer Rosh Yeshiva, explains that the word *simcha* means more than just happiness. Fulfillment is more accurate. "Who is a rich man?" asks the mishnah in *Avos* (4:1), "*Hasamei'ach bechelko* — one who is fulfilled with his share." When Eisav told Yaakov, "I have much," Yaakov responded to his more affluent brother "I have everything." Wealth is relative to our expectations; only if one is satisfied with what he has can he be happy.

For this same reason, explains Rav Samson Raphael Hirsch, there is no official *mitzvah* of *simcha* on Pesach. The Torah commands, "*Vesamachta* — Rejoice" (*Devarim* 16:11,14), both on Sukkos and Shavuos, but not on Pesach. Why? Because Pesach is a reenactment of the exodus from Egypt, when the Jewish people had just been freed from centuries of slavery. While a newly freed slave may be ecstatic with joy, he is far from fulfilled. The fulfillment that is inherent in *simcha* is not yet present. Not until Shavuos, when the Torah is given, can the Jewish people reflect upon their achievements and direct their future. At that point, *simcha* is attainable.

Jewish men, particularly those blessed with the opportunity to be involved in Torah study and communal affairs, feel satisfaction in their work even while they are still single. But with such an outlook, a man is also liable to forget that no matter how talented, how accomplished, how respected he is, fulfillment will not come until after he is married, united with the woman who will join together with him for the rest of his life to make a maximum contribution to this world.

So the *chassan* needs a gentle reminder. That is the *mitzvah* of being *mesamei'ach* him — to impress upon him that as a married man he can now expect fulfillment. By extolling his *kallah,* by noting how suited she is to helping him meet his goals, this is realized. All of his previous accomplishments pale; his real achievements come with her by his side, building a Torah home and family.

By contrast, women are less likely to confuse individual accomplishments with the boundless potential that partnership offers. They know better than to fall prey to the hubris that causes people to inflate the value of individual achievement. Women intuitively sense the greater riches of a couple whose talents and love are dedicated to the pursuit of shared goals. As such, the *kallah* needs no one else to impress these values upon her.

The wedding day shares with Yom Kippur this theme of fulfillment. The forgiveness granted on Yom Kippur provides everyone with an annual second chance to reclaim their potential in Torah and spiritual growth. This is undoubtedly true as well for a *chassan* and *kallah*. Together, on the day of their personal Yom Kippur, they embark on a fresh start, their previous failures and imperfections discarded, ready for the fulfillment of mutual accomplishment.

My dear *chassan* and *kallah,* we rejoice in your new potential. You are uniquely suited to each other, complementing each other's strengths and compensating for each other's weaknesses. May G-d help you reach your potential for accomplishment both personal and communal. May your devotion to each other and to G-d's commands bring the day that will fill our mouths with the song of redemption, when we will all share in the promised *simcha* of Messianic fulfillment.

Sheldon Rudoff

פרשת קדושים
Parshas Kedoshim

IT IS NO COINCIDENCE THAT THE HEBREW WORD for marriage, *kiddushin*, and the name of this week's Torah reading, *Kedoshim*, derive from the same root, *kadosh*. For our Sages have determined to elevate that relationship and assigned *kiddushin* as the name for both the tractate in the Talmud that deals with marriage and the institution that the secular world refers to as "marriage."

In the opening sentences of *Parshas Kedoshim*, the entire congregation of the children of Israel are commanded, "You shall be holy, for I the L-rd, your G-d, am holy" (*Vayikra* 19:2).

What a mind-boggling, challenging concept! Our commentaries from time immemorial have struggled with the staggering idea that equates the holiness of the Jewish people to the holiness of the L-rd. The Midrash explains this connection by stating that holiness connotes separation. But some commentaries, relying upon the many commandments that follow, which take in every facet of human life — agriculture and commerce, war and peace, food and drink, rearing and education of

---

Mr. Rudoff, an attorney, is immediate past president of the Orthodox Union.

children; a complete mixture of mitzvos *bein adam laMakom* and *bein adam lachaveiro*, between man and G-d and between man and his fellow man, tell us that the L-rd, though Omnipotent and separate from the world, is not divorced from it. He is found within the world. And it is Israel's task to emulate the L-rd even in this way: to be holy within the world, to exert our influence and spread His holiness to all areas of life.

Thus, explains the *Kesav Sofer*, the L-rd does not desire one to take on the *kedushah* of *nezirus*, to separate himself from other people in order to perfect only his own soul. Rather, he should benefit others and guide them in how to serve the Holy One. It was for this reason that He gave us Torah and *mitzvos*. For though, "Holy, holy, holy is G-d of Hosts," nevertheless, "the entire world is filled with His glory" (*Yeshayahu* 6:3). What is meant by "You shall be holy" is that Israel must imitate G-d by being a holy nation, not by withdrawing from the world of nations. Israel must radiate a positive influence on the world through every aspect of life and Jewish living. No attempt is made in this parshah to separate the rules governing relations between man and his neighbor and man and his Maker. Both derive from the L-rd's Torah. And both lead to fulfillment of the opening sentence of this *parshah.*

The Midrash, quoted in the first Rashi of the *parshah,* states, "This *parshah* was said in assembly." The commandments contained in this *parshah* differ from all others in the book of *Vayikra*. Only in *Kedoshim* was Moshe commanded to speak to the *entire* congregation of Israel. This was done in order to instruct us that holiness is not based on separation but on assembly — within the congregation and *toch hatzibur*. This notion is so aptly expressed by Rabbi Menachem Mendel of Kotzk, in his inimitable translation of another call to holiness found in the *pasuk,* "*Ve'anshei kodesh tihyun li* — Holy people you shall be to Me" (*Shemos* 22:30). "*Anshei kodesh,*" says the Kotzker, means "*menschlich heilig,*" to be holy in a *menschlich* way, in a manner that is very much attached to humans and humanity.

Undoubtedly, our Sages had this in mind when they decreed that the first step toward marriage is the groom's declaration to his bride that she be "sanctified in accordance with the law of Moshe and Israel." It is a sanctity whose formula is laid out in the fundamental rulings of the Torah contained in *Parshas Kedoshim*. It is the formula with which we charge a new couple as they enter this new phase of their lives which affords each the opportunity to extend to the other the kindness, consideration and love that is implicit in "For I the L-rd, your G-d, am holy."

And not only unto each other but unto the world into which we have been thrust and in which we live. It is a world that often seems so distant from the sanctities of Torah. But it is the world that the L-rd has chosen to fill with His glory. It is the world the L-rd has chosen for us to live in, in a way that reflects His spirit and ennobles mankind.

Surely the most well-known commandment of this *parshah* is, "Love your neighbor as yourself" (*Vayikra* 19:18). Significantly, the Talmud in *Kiddushin* (41a) applies that verse to married love and learns from it the rule that a couple may not marry unless they have first seen and been attracted to each other. Our Sages wisely understood that a match that is based upon mutual feelings of "Love your neighbor as yourself" is also one that can extend beyond that love and into the community and world in which we live.

My dear *chassan* and *kallah,* it is our blessing to you that you fulfill through this union that "great principle of the Torah"; that through mutual love you become sensitive to the needs of each other and *Klal Yisrael;* that through the sanctities that have been entrusted to our nation you create a home and a life which are inextricably tied to the commandment of "*Kedoshim tihiyu* — You shall be holy."

Rabbi Rafael G. Grossman

פרשת אמור
Parshas Emor

פרשת אמור
Parshas Emor

LTHOUGH MARRIED PEOPLE are always eager to share their views on marriage with a new couple, the last thing a *chassan* and *kallah* need is more advice. Just as no two people are alike, no two marriages are identical, and through trial and error each marriage discovers its own personal strengths and weaknesses. One marriage may succeed on the basis of factors that would have little or no benefit for another.

Nonetheless, the Torah does provide a general premise upon which a successful marriage can be achieved. Once this goal is attained, all diversity of personality and conviction finds a place within the immutable Jewish union.

In *Parshas Emor*, G-d ordains laws prohibiting *kohanim* from becoming defiled by the dead. This means that a *kohein* is forbidden not just to touch a corpse, but also to be in the same building as a corpse or to enter a cemetery.

Rabbi Grossman is rav of Baron Hirsch Synagogue in Memphis, Tennessee and president of the Rabbinical Council of America.

But there are exceptions. A *kohein* is allowed — indeed, he is commanded — to become ritually impure by coming into contact with the body of "his flesh that is close to him: to his mother, to his father, to his son, to his daughter, to his brother and to his [unmarried] sister" (*Vayikra* 21:2-3). Curiously, no mention is made in the verse regarding a *kohein's* closest relation, his wife. A literal reading of this verse would lead one to believe that a *kohein* may not attend to his deceased wife.

This is not so, explains the Talmud in *Yevamos* (22b). The term, "his flesh that is close to him," rather than serving as an introduction to the subsequent list of relations specified by the verse, is in fact part of that list. It is a direct reference to his wife. His wife *is* "his flesh that is close to him." This knowledge sheds considerable light upon the Torah's concept of marriage.

Contemporary social thinkers tend to depict marriage as a social contract that results from "falling in love." But marriages based on this idea often fail as love, in our modern milieu, is fleeting and often disappointing.

The Torah, on the other hand, establishes a criterion for marriage that transcends all others. After G-d united Adam with Chavah, the Torah states, "Therefore, man shall leave his father and his mother and cling to his wife, and they will become one flesh" (*Bereishis* 2:24). One flesh: There is no better way to describe the relationship of man and woman in marriage.

The halachic dictum learned from the law of the *kohein* — " 'his flesh': this means his wife" — is the quintessential definition of marriage. A husband and wife are considered by the Torah to be one flesh, a singular being. This bond does not fall away when, for better or worse, conditions change. It holds when the sun shines and when the pall of grief's darkness prevails. When he laughs, she laughs. When she cries, he cries.

At first glance, this unity may appear to come only with the surrender of individuality. But this is not so. Individually, man and woman are incomplete. Only when paired together can they take full advantage of the talents they have been blessed with and the skills they have cultivated.

Our mission as Jews is to emulate G-d. As He is one, so must we be one. This truth reaches exalted levels when that union centers around

Torah and Divine service, for the incorporation of G-d into a marriage elevates all of its elements. Every step taken to fortify the Jewish home and family, every endeavor to advance the cause of Torah and mitzvos confirms one's marriage and replenishes its spirituality.

My dear *chassan* and *kallah,* this sense of unity is all that is needed to build a strong and faithful Jewish home. My fondest gift to you is found in the statement of the twelve tribes to their father, Yaakov: "As there is only One in your heart, so too in our hearts is there only One." Together, may the two of you be one forever.

Rabbi Dr. Herbert C. Dobrinsky

פרשת בהר
Parshas Behar

S HEVA BERACHOS, THE SEVEN BLESSINGS recited while celebrating with a *chassan* and *kallah* during the first seven days of their marriage, are part of a recurring theme in Judaism: the number seven. The seventh day of the world's existence marked the completion of Creation and every seventh day since has been distinguished as the Shabbos, a day not merely of rest but of spiritual revitalization.

Also, every seventh year, the laws of *shemitah* are honored. Jews are prohibited from all manner of agricultural labor in the Holy Land, eating only what the undisturbed earth yields. Even that produce may not be sold and must be given away. The supernatural character of *shemitah* tests one's faith. The sixth year's crop, G-d promises in *Parshas Behar,* will provide not only for that year but for the *shemitah* year and the year following, when planting resumes. But while their land remains fallow, the Jewish people do not. With time off from their labors in the field,

Rabbi Dr. Dobrinsky is vice president for university affairs at Yeshiva University in New York City.

Jews are expected to devote their time to Torah study and spiritual advancement.

The *shemitah* Sabbatical is intended even for those whose careers are dedicated to Torah study, *Nachal Kadumim* contends. He notes that the *amora*, Rava, forbade his students from entering the study hall during the month of Nissan, the height of the harvesting season, and the month of Tishrei, the height of the planting season, in order that they work their fields and maintain their livelihoods for the year. Every year, therefore, even students of Torah lost two months of valuable study time. By the end of six years they were twelve months, or a full year, behind schedule. The *shemitah* year, *Nachal Kadumim* concludes, makes up for that time.

Life's cycle is encapsulated in these sevens. Six days you shall work. Six years you shall sow your field. But the seventh day, the seventh year, is consecrated, set aside for Torah study, devoted to spiritual renewal, to give added strength, sustenance and significance to the next set of days and the next set of years.

Parshas Behar introduces the laws of *shemitah* with the words, "And G-d spoke to Moshe on Mount Sinai saying. . ." (*Vayikra* 25:1). Rashi asks his famous question, "What is the connection between *shemitah* and Sinai? Were not all the *mitzvos* issued from Sinai?" Likewise, one can ask, What is the connection between *shemitah* and the new couple? How does this *parshah* relate to the celebration before us?

Mount Sinai, a low mountain, upon which the Torah was given, evokes the notion of humility. Newlyweds in particular, who must learn to share with each other a life and its concerns, need to act with humility. This is an unerring formula for happiness in a marriage. To address each other's concerns with love and sensitivity — with humility — is to build a unity of spirit that brings into the couple's life the blessings the Torah conferred at Sinai.

Life's mission is presented to the young couple at the beginning of their marriage. They have seven days to celebrate. Like the seventh day of the week and the seventh year of the *shemitah* cycle, these days are devoted exclusively to spiritual renewal, which will provide strength and sustenance for the next cycle of days and years.

The celebration of these seven days of festivities includes the special joy of Shabbos. It is Shabbos that brings to a halt the mundane weekday schedule and replaces it with spiritual rest and replenishment, allowing one's life to be invested with G-d's holy spirit. The "additional soul" that Shabbos provides for each Jew is G-d's special gift to the Jewish people.

For those who are steadfast in their faithfulness to G-d, Shabbos is recognized as a source of both physical and spiritual regeneration. Shabbos is not a day of indolence but a lifeline for sustained growth and motivation as both body and soul are nurtured and blossom in joyous achievement and in the spirit of the Torah's spirituality. Shabbos and *shemitah* gird their adherents with vigor to continue to be creative and productive. The respite from the mundane tasks that life thrusts upon us makes room for, indeed encourages, our spiritual growth — Torah study, *mitzvah* performance — which may have been shortchanged during the weeks and months that have accumulated over the years.

These ideals, encapsulated at the start of marriage, enhance the beauty of the marital relationship, raise it, enable it to transcend its temporal form, and strengthen the bonds of love, loyalty and sanctity which are the hallmarks of every faithful Jewish home and family.

My dear *chassan* and *kallah,* much of our time in this world is spent dealing with the mundane aspects of life, but our infinitely wise Torah provides respites for us along the way. The first week of your marriage is such a period, a time to immerse yourselves in holiness, to prepare for the long, fulfilling, road ahead. By dedicating yourselves to each other and to the building of a Jewish home, a home of Torah, *mitzvos,* kindness and hospitality, you instill sanctity even into those facets of life that appear temporal on the surface. May you be successful on this wondrous journey.

Rabbi Raphael B. Butler

פרשת בחוקותי
Parshas Bechukosai

T HE EXCITEMENT THAT ACCOMPANIES any change in one's life is at its most intense when that change is the entrance into the sacred covenant of marriage. A married couple is as unique as a fingerprint, an unprecedented blend of talents, histories, attitudes and aspirations. As _chassan_ and _kallah_ look toward one another to begin crafting the guidelines for their new life together, they also review their own qualities to see how they will fare in this new relationship. They need look no further than the old standard of commitment to Torah and _mitzvos._

The Midrash, with its interpretive powers, takes the verse in _Parshas Bechukosai_, "If . . . you observe My commands and do them (_vaasisem osam_)" (_Vayikra_ 26:3), and recasts the words to read, "If you observe My commands, then you will make yourselves (_vaasisem atem_)" (_Vayikra Rabbah_ 35:7).

Imagine the sense of pride in creating a human being. Imagine the sense of accomplishment one feels when participating in the process of

Rabbi Butler, rav of the Holliswood Jewish Center in Holliswood, New York, is executive vice president of the Orthodox Union.

creation. G-d informs the Jewish people that they have the opportunity to cast themselves in the role of creator. By following the Torah's instructions for life, Jews literally make themselves — they fashion for themselves a life of spiritual significance.

This opportunity is not limited to the individual person. In building a life based upon Torah and *mitzvos,* a couple, too, cast themselves in the role of creator, not just by physically creating a family but also by infusing that family with the spitituality and sanctity of Torah and the legacy of Sinai.

How appropriate it is then that during these first seven days of marriage, family and friends gather to extol those special qualities of Torah, *mitzvos* and good deeds, which are integral to the personality of the new couple. These celebrations are not simple revelry. Our Sages teach that all who celebrate before the *chassan* and *kallah* are considered to have rebuilt the ruins of Jerusalem (*Berachos* 6b). What is the connection betweeen the two? What message do the Sages wish to impart?

Perhaps this maxim can be interpreted metaphorically. Just as the physical rebuilding of Jerusalem continues with the belief that its *kedushah*, its innate splendor not visible to the naked eye, will blossom, so too the celebration of a new union is carried out with the instinctive belief that the relationship, which is just beginning to take form, will prove to be, after a lifetime of achievement, a splendorous credit to the *kedushah* of the Jewish people.

My dear *chassan* and *kallah,* you join together to create a new, united personality under the direction and inspiration of the Torah. Although your relationship is just beginning to take form, we are confident that you will prove to be a wellspring of Torah, *mitzvos* and good deeds, and that your family will serve as a source of pride for all of *Klal Yisrael.*

ঙ§ *Sefer Bamidbar*

Rabbi Moshe E. Bomzer

פרשת במדבר
Parshas Bamidbar

F
ROM THE FIRST MOMENTS OF MARRIAGE, the focus of one's energies, emotions and interests shift from oneself to incorporate another. "Love your neighbor as yourself" (*Vayikra* 19:18) is never more aptly applied than to a newly married person, as concern for one's personal welfare extends to one's spouse. But how is this verse to be applied? How is this love to be issued?

Parshas Bamidbar opens with G-d commanding Moshe to take a census of the Jewish people. Even though they had just been counted a few months earlier, G-d orders another count. Why the need for another tally? Rashi explains: "Because they are beloved before Him, he counts them every hour" (*Bamidbar* 1:1). While "every hour" may be hyperbolic, the phrase nevertheless conveys the manner in which G-d confers love upon his people and, consequently, how His subjects should confer love upon each other.

Rashi lists the number of times mentioned in the Torah that G-d counted His people: He counted them when they left Egypt, after they

---

Rabbi Bomzer is rav of Congregation Beth Abraham Jacob in Albany, New York.

worshipped the Golden Calf, and after the Tabernacle was erected and dedicated. These times represent different moments in Jewish history — times of national upheaval, times of wretched failure, times of sterling achievement. There were times in Jewish history when the Jews were counted following noble and beautiful acts. G-d's love was apparent.

But just the same, there were moments when they betrayed G-d's trust and deserved to lose His affection. Nonetheless, love was still forthcoming. G-d again counted them. In good times and in bad times, G-d counts the Jewish people. Regardless of time, place and circumstance, G-d engages in the loving act of counting His people. G-d's love for the Jewish nation is unconditional and thus serves as a paradigm for marriage.

A newly married couple must follow G-d's example and pledge unconditional love to each other. This noble idea is illustrated by the *halachah* that states that the wedding band that the *chassan* gives his *kallah* under the *chuppah* be unadorned. "The custom is to marry with a ring that has no stone" (*Even Ha'ezer* 31:2). Why is that? Because a precious stone in the ring may cause the *kallah* to overestimate its value and consequently consent to marriage based on the false impression that she is marrying a wealthy man. This could invalidate the *kiddushin* and the marriage would be in question. For the contract of *kiddushin* to occur, a meeting of the minds is necessary; any misconception could void the marriage.

But there is another, deeper, symbolic message found in the wedding band. When a precious stone is damaged it can never be repaired. It can be redesigned perhaps, but the flaw remains forever embedded in the stone. But a plain metal band, if damaged, is unlike a stone; it can always be reshaped and restored to its original appearance.

If one were to compare a couple's marriage to a diamond, any defect in the marriage would necessarily be viewed as a permanent flaw, one that could not be ameliorated, one that could not be overcome by compromise and love. Marriages, therefore, should not be likened to a stone. The difficulties of marriage are not intractable. Through love and devotion, husband and wife can repair all the blemishes their relationship may be faced with. Their bond is like a plain band. It can always be repaired, and like G-d's love for his people, their love should never be flawed or withheld.

My dear *chassan* and *kallah,* each of you brings to this marriage extraordinary talents, *middos* and love. Certainly there will be times when crises arise, when the shine and sparkle of your union will become tarnished. But you will be able to repair those moments by recalling the nature of G-d's love for his nation — unconditional — and by incorporating that type of love into your marriage.

"Because of His love for them, He counts them every hour." G-d counts each and every one of us, says the *Keli Yakar,* because each of us has a distinct destiny, a *hashgachah peratis,* an individual connection to G-d and a unique mission to fulfill. By emulating G-d, by emulating His love, you will be on the road to accomplishing that mission, and you will insure that G-d shall forever dwell in your midst and bestow upon you blessings of joy and success each and every day.

Rabbi David Stavsky

פרשת נשא
Parshas Naso

I N THE PARSHAH OF *NASO*, Hashem tells Moshe, "Count (*Naso*) the heads of the children of Gershon . . .."

This word *Naso* has a number of translations. *Naso* means "count." *Naso* also means "lift up" or "elevate," and it also means "carry."

One can elaborate on this word, *naso*, as it relates to the marriage that we are celebrating this week.There are, in fact, three words which describe the marriage institution.

The first is *erusin*, which means to bind up, or tie. The second is *nessuin*, which mean to elevate, and the final word is *kedushin*, which means to sanctify.

Your marriage has three stages. The first was *erusin*, the knots, the ties, the bonds of friendship. You met at *shul* or school or elsewhere and you developed a friendship. The knot of friendship was tied with mutual affection and devotion.

Rabbi Stavsky is rav of Congregation Beth Jacob in Columbus, Ohio.

Then came *nessuin*. You "elevated" each other in your eyes and hearts. You began "counting" on each other . You knew also that each of you "counts" as an individual and has a special meaning in life. You also began to "carry" each other's burdens.

And now with the *chuppah* ceremony celebrated, your mutual goal of *kedushin* has been met. Sanctify your marriage. Sanctify it with a sacred commitment to each other. Sanctify it with making Hashem, Torah, and *mitzvos* part of your new house. Remain the *"rei'im ha'ahuvim,"* the perfect loving friends who began a courtship.

My dear *chassan* and *kallah,* continuously elevate each other in your hearts, carry each other's burdens, and count on each other. Be blessed with a sanctification and purity of your home, reflecting that G-d's *Shechinah* indeed dwells with you and always blesses you.

Dr. Michael Kram

פרשת נשא
Parshas Naso

THE _PARSHAH_ OF _NASO_ HAS THE DISTINCTION of being read on the Shabbos before Shavuos, the holiday that celebrates the marriage of the Jewish people to G-d and to the Torah. The Hebrew word for marriage, _nissuin_, shares its root with the word _naso_, and true to its roots, the _parshah_ contains a valuable message for every chassan and _kallah._

Among the _mitzvos_ documented in _Parshas Naso_ are the procedures for dealing with the adultery of the _sotah_ and the teetotalism of the _nazir_. The juxtaposition of these two ideas is not coincidental; the Talmud links them. "Why is the section of _nazir_ placed next to the section of _sotah_? To tell you that whoever sees a _sotah_ in her disgrace should estrange himself from wine, for it leads to adultery" (_Sotah_ 2a).

Ironically, wine is also used to sanctify every significant Jewish occasion. A _kos shel berachah_ — a cup of wine over which blessings are said — is enlisted for, among other events, _kiddush_ on Shabbos and the

---

Dr. Kram is a practicing gastroenterologist from Monsey, New York.

136 / SASON VESIMCHA

Festivals, *birkas hamazon*, *bris milah*, the Pesach *seder,* weddings and *sheva berachos*.

This is the dual function of wine — it can be used to lift up and it can be used to bring down. Wine, which is used to sanctify a wedding, can also be the downfall of a marriage, as in the case of the *sotah*. The very beverage that is employed to elevate a union contains the potency to tear that union apart.

The paradoxical nature of wine is embodied in the word *naso*, which can be translated both as "raise" and as "remove." From the moment they leave the *chuppah,* a couple must continually work on raising the level of their relationship to achieve a positive *nissuin*. If they do not, they risk the adverse meaning of *naso*, G-d forbid, feeling removed from each other.

When two people marry, each becomes closer than ever before to another human being, a closeness that can be a source of love or a source of strife. Each partner must therefore toil to embrace the former and shun the latter. The term in *Bereishis* (2:18) used to describe Chavah is *"eizer kenegdo,"* a helper opposite Adam. Rabbi Elazar gives a more sobering translation of the term: "If he is worthy, she is his helper; if he is not worthy, she is opposite him," she is his adversary (*Yevamos* 63a).

How does he become worthy? He must be blessed, and to understand how he achieves that blessing, he should look immediately after the section dealing with the *nazir*, where the Torah reveals how the Jewish people are to be blessed. Three verses compose the blessing that the *kohanim* pronounce upon the Jewish people and which are said every day in the morning prayers. Each of these three verses, according to the Midrash as interpreted by the *Torah Temimah*, represents a different type of blessing.

The first verse, *"Yivarechecha Hashem veyishmerecha* — G-d should bless you and guard you" (*Bamidbar* 6:24), is a blessing for material wealth. "May G-d bless you with money and guard you — that you should use your money for charity," says the Midrash. What is the connection to charity? Rashi explains, "One who wants to preserve his money should always give it away to charity, for giving it away preserves it" (*Kesubos* 66b). By investing their material blessings in charitable causes, a couple guarantees their blessing will remain with them.

Money that is spent on the pursuit of materialism is gone. Money that is spent on Divine service remains forever.

The second verse, *"Ya'eir Hashem panav eilecha viychuneka — May G-d shine His countenance upon you and show you favor"* (6:25), is a blessing for spiritual achievement. *"Ya'eir — Shine — this is the light of Torah" (Sifri 41).* The Torah is what illuminates the world, showing us the way to behave even in the darkest times. G-d's "countenance," explains the Netziv in his commentary on the *Sifri,* means His method for running the world, and that is found in the Torah. The Torah is our blueprint for successful passage through this world.

The third verse, *"Yisa Hashem panav eilecha veyaseim lecha shalom — May G-d raise His countenance toward you and bring you peace"* (6:26), is a blessing even for those times when we don't deserve it. These are times when G-d treats us *lifnim meshuras hadin,* above the line of the law. G-d raises us above our sins and saves us from the danger that we place ourselves in.

My dear *chassan* and *kallah,* life continually places obstacles in our paths. These obstacles can be seen as challenges and opportunities for growth, for *eizer,* or they can be used as excuses for friction, for *kenegdo.* It is in your power as husband and wife to take everything in this world and elevate each one, to respond to every action with a positive reaction. Your families and friends are confident that the wine over which we make the seven blessings will be a harbinger of the holiness that will occupy your home, a home of Torah and a home of charity, and mark the start of a union that is forever blessed both materially and spiritually. "May G-d raise His countenance toward you and bring you peace."

Rabbi Eliezer Langer

פרשת בהעלותך
Parshas Beha'aloscha

ONE NEED NOT HAVE ATTENDED the *bris* of the *chassan* to know that after he was named, those in attendance proclaimed with great joy, "Just as he has entered into the covenant, so may he enter into Torah, *chuppah* and good deeds." This blessing was also given to the *kallah's* parents after she was named: "May you raise her to Torah, *chuppah* and good deeds."

One must wonder about the sequence of this benediction, puzzled that *chuppah* is sandwiched between the other two. Do Torah and good deeds not play vital roles in a Jew's life prior to marriage as well as after? Why not mention *chuppah* first? Or last? what is the reason for placing it in the middle?

The *Kesav Sofer* deciphers this sequence by pointing out that it is the obligation of parents to provide their children with a Torah education. *Halachah* clearly defines the stages of training that children must go through as they grow up and develop, and the mishnah in *Avos* (5:25) gives guidelines for the progression of a child's course of study: at five, he begins learning Scripture; at ten, Mishnah; at fifteen, Talmud.

Rabbi Langer is rav of Congregation Beth Jacob, in San Diego, California.

It is this training that remains rooted in every Jew forever. Although Jews must study Torah throughout their lifetimes and their understanding of Jewish law, philosophy and ethics is shaped by life's experiences, they are nevertheless indelibly marked by the education they received as children in the care of their parents. The Torah one learns as a child forges his perspective on Judaism for life.

With respect to good deeds, however, the opposite is true. Albeit correct behavior and kindness must be taught and demonstrated by parents, it is only later in life, after having matured, that children begin to perform good deeds out of the kindness of their own hearts. After marriage, this kindness develops even further. A couple can create an independent base from which *chessed* can flow, a home in which the training of their parents can blossom into heartfelt deeds. Together, they have the responsibility to care selflessly for each other and have the ability to forge a home that is open to others.

Moreover, one's level of kindness can mature even during marriage. Rav Henoch Leibowitz defines two types of kindness. One is based on the compassion one has for a fellow human being, in which case the recipient feels indebted to his benefactor. The other stems from a feeling of mutual love, in which case the beneficiary does not feel lessened by the experience. He feels a sense of camaraderie rather than a sense of inferiority. It is a more refined way of distributing kindness when, although one party is giving, the other does not feel he is taking.

This superior stage of kindness is demonstrated by G-d when He instructs Aharon in the lighting of the Menorah in the Tabernacle. The Midrash records a conversation between the Jews and G-d. The Jews were perplexed by this *mitzvah* and asked, "Master of the universe, You ask us to make light for You? You are the light of the world!"

G-d replies, "It is not that I need [light from] you, but you should light for Me as I lit [the way in the wilderness] for you. Why? To elevate you before the other nations, who will say, 'Look how Israel lights for He Who lights up the world.' "

The Midrash then brings a parable. A sighted man was leading a blind man along the road. "When we get to the house," the sighted man said to the blind man, "go and light this candle for me and give me light so that you will not owe me a favor on account of my having led you on the road" (*Bamidbar Rabbah* 15:4).

By commanding the Jewish people to light the Menorah for Him, G-d shows the world that He acts on our behalf not out of pity but out of a mutual love in which both parties give.

Upon leaving the *chuppah*, a couple departs with the opportunity to engage in the highest level of kindness — mutual giving propelled by love. When their home is established upon this foundation of kindness, their good deeds are accomplished on the higher of the two levels, generated by the new attitudes that marriage produces.

My dear *chassan* and *kallah*, you have just achieved the second stage of the three-faceted blessing bestowed upon you at birth. You now have both Torah and *chuppah*. From this day forward you begin to achieve the third stage, loving kindness, giving of yourselves to each other, to your family, to your community and to your nation. Our wish is for you to have a long, fruitful life together in which to realize this goal and embellish it with your unique skills and talents. In that way, you will honor your Torah education and your marriage, and, like the Menorah, you will radiate a light that will serve as an example and shine upon us all.

Rabbi Dr. Joseph I. Singer

פרשת שלח
Parshas Shelach

STANDING NEXT TO EACH OTHER under the *chuppah,* a *chassan* and *kallah* are at the end of one journey and about to embark upon another. Their first journey began with their introduction to each other, continued through a period of courtship and engagement, and successfully culminated in marriage. Each partner has found in the other a companion and a soul-mate with whom to share a life.

Together they now commence a new journey, that of building a Jewish home and family. To help them on their way to their personal promised land, one finds it valuable to glean some of the lessons learned from our nation's trek to our national promised land, Eretz Yisrael.

Parshas Shelach tells of the historic expedition dispatched by Moshe to explore the Holy Land. Twelve leaders of Israel, one from each tribe, were chosen to scout the land and returned with a disparaging report,

---

Rabbi Singer is rabbi emeritus of the Manhattan Beach Jewish Center in Brooklyn, New York.

discouraging the nation from entering the land and establishing for themselves an infamous reputation as *meraglim*, which has lasted throughout Jewish history.

Only two of the spies, Yehoshua and Caleiv, returned with an optimistic and uplifting account of the land. Although all the others disputed their claims, they were steadfast. These two heroes were able to stand up to the majority of their peers and speak the truth. What was the secret of their success? How did they carry out their mission properly while their colleagues failed?

The answer lies in their vision. Yehoshua and Caleiv shared a perspective of the situation that was different from the perspective of the other ten. The *meraglim* told the Jewish nation, "The land that we passed through to explore her is a land that eats her inhabitants" (*Bamidbar* 14:32). Every place they went, Rashi explains, they saw the Canaanites burying their dead; this was a dangerous place to live, they concluded. But what they did not perceive was that G-d had arranged for many funerals to take place on that day so that the twelve explorers would be able to move around unnoticed.

The *meraglim* missed the point. They were impressed by what they saw with their eyes: huge, fortified cities; great warriors; formidable terrain. Yehoshua and Caleiv, on the other hand, saw beyond what was visible to the naked eye. They understood what could only be seen by an inner eye, one that looks beyond the shallow facade of life, one that penetrates the surface and sees the deeper significance of events. The pair subordinated sight to insight. While sight senses only appearance, insight perceives reality.

What was it specifically that they perceived? Referring to the inhabitants of Canaan, Yehoshua and Caleiv told the Jewish people, "Do not fear the people of the land. . .their security has left them and G-d is with us; do not fear them" (14:9). Rashi notes that "their security" refers to G-d's protection. With G-d, one has security; without Him, one has nothing. Yehoshua and Caleiv were secure in their knowledge that the Jewish people would conquer the land as G-d had promised them. They knew they could never fail by following G-d's instruction.

The *meraglim* were not as confident. "All those men who saw My glory and My miracles that I did in Egypt and in the wilderness . . . and they did not listen to My voice" (14:22). And so G-d banned them and the entire generation from the Promised Land. For though they saw with their eyes what G-d could do, they were still capable of not listening to Him.

When two people unite in marriage to create a Jewish home and further the Jewish mission, they secure Divine protection. Like Yehoshua and Caleiv, who banded together in their mutual conviction of the truth, who saw beyond the surface, who listened to G-d, this couple can not fail. With a common resolve they can go against the grain of a society that is often at odds with Torah values, and they can build a future together of spiritual and material success.

My dear *chassan* and *kallah,* marriage may be based on love and commitment, but it is fortified by character, ambition, heritage and a capacity to see the eternal amid the fleeting. The insight of two people bound to Torah is stronger than the false visions of society's multitudes. As long as G-d is with you in building a Jewish home, there is nothing to fear. As you take your first steps in marriage, may you always overcome obstacles, be immune to negativism, and go forward together, hand in hand and heart to heart, toward your promised land.

Rabbi Alan Kalinsky

פרשת קרח
Parshas Korach

I N *PARSHAS KORACH*, THE TORAH INTRODUCES the action of a man and his 250 followers as the paradigm of rebellion. Korach and his cohorts are envious of Moshe and Aharon and their roles as the heads of the Jewish people, positions they feel they themselves deserve.

At first glance, the picture of Korach and his crew comes across as evil, in light of their mutiny against Moshe. But the Torah informs us that these were no ordinary men. They were among the greatest Jews of their generation and, nonetheless, they sinned, they overstepped their bounds. "You have taken upon yourselves a great responsibility" (*Bamidbar* 16:7), Moshe informs them, and Rashi adds, "to contest with the L-rd." In challenging Moshe's authority, his leadership of the Jewish people, Korach and his men challenged G-d's choice of Moshe as His supreme prophet.

The mishnah in *Avos* (5:20) teaches that an argument made for the sake of Heaven will endure. Why? Because, explains the Rambam, the argument is being presented in order to reach a truthful conclusion. The

---

Rabbi Kalinsky is West Coast director of the Orthodox Union.

famous disputes between Hillel and Shamai are named by the mishnah as the quintessential example of this form of argumentation. To this day, though the halachah generally sides with Hillel, both positions are noted and both are discussed.

The dissension of Korach, on the other hand, is the mishnah's example of the type of argument that does not endure. While Moshe and Aharon were vindicated, Korach and his followers were vanquished. Korach's contention is recorded in a negative light and his claim is never again taken seriously. When the search for truth is absent and replaced by the pursuit of self-interest, G-d punishes quickly and severely.

Still there was one man, counted initially in Korach's camp, who was not punished. On ben Peles, named at the beginning of the *parshah* as a co-conspirator of Korach's, is never mentioned again in the *parshah.* The Torah details the fate of Dassan and Aviram. The Torah details the fate of the other members of the rebellion. But On mysteriously disappears from further mention. What happened to him?

The Midrash fills in his story: On's wife foresaw the tragic consequences of Korach's behavior and was intent on stopping her husband before he became further entangled with this group. "Why are you involved in this dispute?" she reasoned with him. "If Aharon is the *kohein gadol,* you are a subordinate and if Korach is the *kohein gadol,* you are a subordinate."

But On felt trapped. He had committed himself to the cause. "What should I do?" he asked his wife.

She had a plan. She gave him wine, got him drunk and put him to bed. When the other men came to collect him, she subtly discouraged them from entering the house and they left. While he slept, the others were killed, swallowed into the ground. Due to his wife's persistence, On survived while Korach — who was provoked by *his* wife into challenging Moshe — perished. Thus the Midrash, quoting the verse in *Mishlei* (14:1), states, " 'The wisdom of woman builds her home' — this is the wife of On; 'and foolishness with her hands will demolish it' — this is the wife of Korach" (*Bamidbar Rabbah* 18:15). Two marriages with two very different results.

Every marriage experiences challenges and crises. How husband and wife react to them will determine whether they survive or succumb. If a spouse is determined to hold his ground, as Korach did, without a willingness to compromise, success in marriage is unlikely. If, on the other hand, a spouse is willing to look for a solution to remedy the situation, as On's wife did, success in marriage is guaranteed.

When self-interest is put aside, when partners look at every situation objectively, with an open mind and are willing to follow the example of On and his wife and retreat on a previous stance, their marriage will endure. Indeed, tempered by the experience, it will become stronger, just as the arguments between Hillel and Shamai served to strengthen rather than weaken the cause of Torah.

My dear *chassan* and *kallah,* you are both committed to each other and to G-d's Torah and *mitzvos,* you are committed to seeking the truth in all areas of life, you are committed to turning disagreements into agreements. By adhering to these commitments and combining them with love, care and trust, you will be creating a Jewish home that will provide you and your families with much to take pride in.

Rabbi Sidney Shoham

פרשת חקת
Parshas Chukas

G-D TELLS HIS PEOPLE, "I will betroth you to Me forever" (*Hoshei'a* 2:21). When a *chassan* gives his ring to the *kallah* he creates a similar bond, a bond of eternal commitment. Marriage is as sanctified an act of endless devotion as was found at Sinai.

Moshe's relationship to the Jewish people was similarly one of endless commitment. He led them through forty tumultuous years in the wilderness, a period that had its ups and downs. Was there a more thrilling moment than the revelation of G-d at Sinai? Was there a more frustrating moment than the mutiny of Korach? Moshe's tenure comprised four decades that combined spiritual ecstasy with mortal rejection. There were daily miracles of bread, shelter and clothing and there were periodic grievances over meat, safety, and in *Parshas Chukas*, water.

When the Jewish people complain about a lack of water in the wilderness, G-d commands Moshe and Aharon to speak to a rock, which

---

Rabbi Shoham is rav of the Beth Zion Congregation in Cote St. Luc, Quebec.

was to produce water for the nation. But instead, Moshe hits the rock. Subsequently, he and Aharon are denied entry into the land of Israel "because you did not trust in Me to sanctify Me in the eyes of the children of Israel" (*Bamidbar* 20:12).

In one short verse, our hero becomes a victim. One reads the verse and comes away shattered and bewildered. How could it be that Moshe, who had done so much for the Jewish people, is denied such a great privilege for what seems a minor infraction? What exactly did he do wrong?

Although the verse does not pinpoint Moshe's sin, the most apparent explanation for his punishment is the one Rashi gives, that by hitting the rock rather than speaking to it, Moshe defied the will of G-d. Had Moshe and Aharon spoken to the rock as G-d instructed, G-d's Name would have been sanctified before the nation. The people would have thought, "Just as this rock, which does not speak, does not hear, and does not require sustenance, fulfills the word of the Eternal, certainly we should."

But the Ramban is troubled by this explanation. He points out that since G-d instructed Moshe to "take the staff" (20:8) when approaching the rock, the implication was to use it, as he had used it in Egypt to initiate the plagues.

The Ramban, therefore, prefers Rabbeinu Chananel's reading of this incident, that Moshe's mistake came before he hit the rock. After receiving G-d's instruction on how to draw out the water, Moshe and Aharon gathered the Jewish people around the rock and asked them, "Hear, you rebels, shall we bring forth for you water from this rock?" (20:10). By including the word "we" in this rhetorical question, they emphasized their own role in the miracle and missed an opportunity to glorify G-d and His wonders.

The Rambam in *Shemoneh Perakim* (4) offers a third opinion. Moshe erred when he addressed the Jews as rebels. His show of irritation was — for a man of Moshe's stature — a desecration of G-d's Name. The Jewish people looked toward Moshe's example for instruction on proper behavior and as their role model he should have displayed more patience.

There are other interpretations. The commentaries combine to offer over a dozen different explanations to these few verses, and although no consensus is reached, many lessons are learned. Rashi teaches that following G-d's direction means physical abuse can never replace the power of the spoken word. The Ramban emphasizes the need to give credit to whom it is due. And the Rambam embraces the significance of staying calm in stressful situations and that how you say something is as important as the content of what you say.

These lessons are never more fitting than for a *chassan* and *kallah*. From Rashi they are taught to shun any type of physical abuse. Talking things out can accomplish everything. From the Ramban they are taught to give each other their due recognition. They should not shy away from complimenting and thanking each other regularly, and certainly not take credit away from each other. From the Rambam they are taught that everlastiong love calls for a world of patience and sympathetic control of one's language. Verbal abuse is not an option.

My dear *chassan* and *kallah*, despite his greatness, Moshe was refused entry into Eretz Yisrael because he slipped in the aforementioned areas. You must learn from his mistake. May your home be filled with eternal bliss and commitment by simply loving each other without abusing each other, by appreciating each other for who you are, and by having the patience of Job to reach your Garden of Eden on this world.

Rabbi Dov Eliyahu Leff

פרשת בלק
Parshas Balak

T

HE *PARSHAH* OF *BALAK* contains one of the most well-known verses in the Torah, quoting not G-d or Moshe but the gentile prophet, Bilam, who unwittingly blesses the Jewish people. His words have been incorporated into the *siddur,* a blessing repeated every morning and one familiar to even the youngest Jewish children: "*Mah tovu ohalecha Yaakov, mishkenosecha Yisrael —* How good are your tents, Yaakov, your residences, Yisrael" (*Bamidbar* 24:5). Bilam's praise of both tents and residences is not reduntant, not merely a poetic device. His message is indeed twofold.

What is the difference between an *ohel,* a tent, and a *mishkan,* a residence? A tent is a temporary home; a residence is a permanent one. While the *ohel* represents the temporal, material, fleeting aspects of this world, the *mishkan* represents the spiritual, sanctified, enduring side of life. The *ohel* represents a Jew's journey into secular society, where, though he functions under the standard of *derech eretz*, his participation

Rabbi Leff is a senior director of the Orthodox Union's synagogue services department and editor of **Torah Insights**.

is still temporary. For a lifestyle that secures a future, that is rooted, he must draw back into the *mishkan*, into the sanctuary of Torah life, the place of eternal values. This is the Jew's genuine home.

This dichotomy between the spiritual and the material is also reflected in the verse's use of our Patriarch's two names. The name Yaakov was given to him because, as he and his twin brother entered this world, "his hand held on to the heel (*eikev*) of Eisav" (*Bereishis* 25:26). Coming out of the womb, Yaakov tried to restrain Eisav. He tried to prevent him from dominating the physical world. His name, Yaakov, applies to his physical nature and, accordingly, to the physical side of the Jewish people.

Later in life, Yaakov was renamed Yisrael, after wrestling through the night with the angel of Eisav. Theirs was a spiritual battle, a battle that Yisrael won. The spiritual side of the Jewish people is therefore represented by the name Yisrael. Bilam thus compliments both Yaakov's *ohel*, his physical side, and Yisrael's *mishkan*, his spiritual pursuit.

As the faithful Jew encounters the *ohel* of secular society, he must guard himself against the forces of Eisav. Like Yisrael of old, he must be strong and fully committed to the *mishkan* of Torah in order to prevent the fleeting values of Eisav to dominate him.

How can one be victorious over the values of Eisav? How does one transform his *ohel*, his physical surroundings into an *ohel* of Torah — a *mishkan*? By again following the footsteps of our forefather. "And Yaakov was an ordinary man, living in tents" (25:27). Which tents? "The tent of Sheim and the tent of Eiver," the two leading Torah scholars of his generation, Rashi explains.

With a commitment to learning and observing Torah, today's Jew can also dwell in a *mishkan*, a place of G-d, a home wherein the sanctified, eternal values of the Jewish faith dominate.

In the Talmud (*Sanhedrin* 105b), Rabbi Yochanan extracts from the blessings that Bilam offered the Jewish people the various curses that he had intended to cast upon them. Rabbi Abba bar Kahana adds that all these curses were in fact fulfilled eventually, when the Jewish people sinned. All but one. Their houses of worship and halls of study were never shut down. The inadvertent blessing of "*Mah tovu ohalecha Yaakov, mishkenosecha Yisrael*" was never reversed. Why?

The *Torah Temimah* explains that since the world's existence is dependent on Torah study and the perpetuation of the Torah's mission, it is impossible for this blessing to ever be undone.

My dear *chassan* and *kallah*, both of you live in two worlds, the world of the *ohel* and the world of the *mishkan*. Both of you understand the disparity between ephemeral secular values and eternal Torah values, as your commitment to Torah learning and Torah observance testifies. At the same time, you have not divorced yourselves from *derech eretz*, from your careers and your involvement in American society, but always with the understanding that your professions are just an *ohel*, while Torah Judaism remains your *mishkan*, your permanent residence.

To you we proclaim, "How good is your *ohel*," your involvement in the world and humanity, and "How good is your *mishkan*," your dedication to G-d, his people and the land of Israel. May G-d bless your new home, your new personal *mishkan*, and forever keep a presence there in fulfilling the verse, "And they will make for me a sanctuary and I will dwell among them" (*Shemos* 25:8).

Rabbi Zvi Karpel

Parshas Pinchas

P ARSHAS PINCHAS OUTLINES some of the exemplary qualities that a couple need to develop while they set out to build a new home. The *parshah* begins with Pinchas receiving a hero's welcome from G-d for his decisive action — killing a Jewish dignitary so that G-d's honor would be preserved in front of the entire nation of Israel. "Behold I present to him My pact of peace," G-d tells Moshe (*Bamidbar* 25:12). Pinchas had the strength to ignore the prince's high position and risked his life to protect the sanctity of Torah's values.

Another enlightening episode in this *parshah* is the case of Zelaphchad's daughters. Zelaphchad died without sons and Jewish law stipulates that only sons inherit their father's possessions. Nevertheless, his daughters argued, since their father left no male heirs, they should inherit his share in the land of Israel. The women were not afraid to approach Moshe with their claim and their courage was vindicated. Not only was their contention correct, but they immortalized themselves.

Rabbi Karpel is chaplain of the Daughters of Israel Geriatric Center in West Orange, New Jersey.

Their names are listed in the Torah and are forever associated with this law of inheritance. "The daughters of Zelaphchad were meritorious and [the law] was written by their hand," the Talmud states (*Sanhedrin* 8a).

Moshe also displays courage in this incident. Though he had already determined that the women's argument was logically sound, he deferred to G-d for the answer. The Midrash (*Bamidbar Rabbah* 21:13) points out that Zelaphchad's daughters initially approached the lower courts of Jewish law for a ruling, but those courts felt unqualified to decide the case and so deferred it to the higher courts. These courts too felt themselves to be unqualified and the matter reached Moshe. But he too did not want to pronounce the law on his own. "Moshe saw that every one [of the courts] honored the one greater than it. He reasoned, If I tell them the law, I will receive the glory. [Instead] he told them, Even I have Someone greater than me. 'And Moshe brought their case before the L-rd' (*Bamidbar* 27:5)." Moshe demonstrated before the entire nation that one ought not hesitate in seeking the guidance of a higher authority, even when he believes he has the correct answer.

A newly married couple, sure to face important issues and difficult decisions in the years ahead, would be wise to adopt the characteristics of Moshe, Pinchas and Zelaphchad's daughters. They must hold the integrity of the Torah, with its laws and its values, as paramount, and have the courage to uphold that integrity. In building a family, a home of Torah, the attitude of Pinchas is necessary. When the values of society do not mesh with our own, Jews must be strong and resolute in their resistance. The Torah's honor is not negotiable. This message is especially important when transmitting Torah values to children.

Husband and wife would also benefit from following Moshe's example and always consulting each other — and others, when necessary — on important matters. Even when you think you have the answer, even when your conclusion is logically sound, it never hurts to get a second opinion, especially the opinion of your spouse.

Finally, when facing something they feel strongly about, a couple should not sit back. They should pursue it as the daughters of Zelaphchad pursued their case. More often that not, the result will be positive.

There is one more distinction to *Parshas Pinchas*. Physically, it is the most worn part of a Torah scroll. Since *Pinchas* details the special sacrifices brought in the Temple on Rosh Chodesh, the Festivals, Rosh Hashanah and Yom Kippur, those sections of the *parshah* are read on their corresponding days. The verses of *Pinchas* are thus read more frequently than any other *parshah's* and, consequently, the parchment upon which those verses are written suffer more wear and tear than other sections of the Torah. The *parshah* also describes the two offerings brought daily as well as on Shabbos. Thus, we turn to *Parshas Pinchas* regularly throughout the year; it is relevant every day of the Jewish calendar.

My dear *chassan* and *kallah, Parshas Pinchas* corresponds to your life together. As you go through life there will be much wear and tear, many trials and challenges in the process. But your connection to Torah provides you with daily, weekly, monthly and yearly reminders of your relationship to G-d and His commands. We pray that you will be blessed with the courage of Pinchas, the determination of Zelaphchad's daughters, and the humility of Moshe — all of which will enable you not only to persevere, but to develop spiritually and offer strength to each other, to your families and to *Klal Yisrael.*

Rabbi Mordechai Willig

פרשת מטות־מסעי
Parshas Mattos-Masei

A CCORDING TO ASHKENAZIC CUSTOM, weddings do not take place during the week of *Parshas Matos-Masei* because it falls during the three-week period commemorating the *Churban*, the destruction of our Holy Temple in Jerusalem. For couples wed before these three weeks, however, *sheva berachos* celebrations are held during this week, and at such a time, with the confluence of these two disparate events, it is most appropriate to understand the lessons of our national history in general and the *Churban* in particular, and to apply those lessons to our *chassan* and *kallah* as they set out together to build their home in Israel.

The Talmud teaches that Jerusalem was destroyed because, although Jews were observant of G-d's commands, they refused to go beyond the letter of the law in dealing with fellow Jews (*Bava Metzia* 30b). Elsewhere, the Talmud teaches that the destruction came about because *sinas chinam*, baseless hatred, was rampant among the Jewish

---

Rabbi Willig is rav of the Young Israel of Riverdale and a rosh yeshiva at Yeshivat Rabbenu Yitzchak Elchanan in New York City.

people (*Yoma* 9b). Tosafos concludes that it was both these factors that combined to bring on the *Churban*.

But one can also understand these two traits as being one. What the Talmud calls *sinas chinam* is generally understood as baseless hatred. However, hatred is never entirely baseless. There is always some offense, however slight, that initially triggers and then feeds one person's dislike of another. Still, the Talmud judges this hatred to be baseless, because a person should be able to overlook these slight offenses and petty grievances.

What allowed *sinas chinam* to infiltrate the Jewish community and lead to the *Churban*? The Jews' insistence on following the letter of the law. Since the Jews of that time refused to give their fellow Jews any latitude, grudges began and festered. One's refusal to forgive another's minor indiscretion swelled into full-blown hatred. In this manner, unjustified hatred stemmed from self-imposed limits on human kindness and understanding. In time, this attitude cost the Jewish people their Holy Temple.

Moshe himself lamented this attitude in *Parshas* Devarim. "*Eichah esa levadi torchachem masachem verivchem*," he tells the Jewish people. "How can I alone carry your troubles, your burdens and your disputes?" (*Devarim* 1:12). He begins with "*Eichah*," the very word repeated in the book of *Eichah*, read at the conclusion of the Three Weeks, on the blackest day of the Jewish year, Tisha B'Av. When this verse is read on the Shabbos before Tisha B'Av, as it is every year, the reader reads it with the same traditional mournful tune of *Megilas Eichah*. Moshe's lament is tied to the *Churban* by more than just a common word.

Rashi details Moshe's complaint. The Jews who came to him with their cases insisted upon their legal rights to adduce more proofs, summon additional witnesses, even increase the number of judges when they sensed a decision not going in their favor. These maneuvers, while technically legal, undermined the friendship and respect that are prerequisites for Jewish society to function properly. With that element missing, no judge, not even Moshe, could ably handle the troubles, burdens and disputes that face any society. When that element is missing, the collapse of society is imminent and there is no room for a Temple.

The Jewish home is a microcosm of both the Temple and Jewish society. As such, a new *chassan* and *kallah* must be mindful of our people's history and learn its timeless lesson: Nobody's perfect. The key to a successful marriage is the willingness to overlook each other's imperfections.

This attitude is particularly needed in the initial stages of married life. When two people get married and establish a home together, each of them inevitably discovers something about the other. Personal habits and private domestic conduct are, by definition, unknown until after the wedding. During the periods of courtship and engagement, people are careful to exhibit exemplary behavior. Anger is controlled. Courtesy and etiquette are fully observed. It is only after the wedding that people let their guard down and only then are their shortcomings revealed.

What is the Torah's response to this problem? Perhaps the answer lies in a special dispensation granted to a *chassan* during the week of his *sheva berachos*. The Talmud teaches that we should not examine his *nega'im* to determine if they are symptomatic of the plague of *tzaraas* (*Mo'eid Katan* 7b). Usually, this law is explained by comparing the festive week of marriage to a Yom Tov. The Torah does not wish to spoil a holiday.

However, a different explanation can be offered: A *chassan* must overlook the shortcomings of his new wife. This obligation corresponds to, and is inferred from, the Torah's command to overlook the *chassan's nega'im*, which represent his imperfections. In fact, some authorities cite this rarely applied *halachah* as the Torah source for the *mitzvah* of *simchas chassan vekallah*, the requirement for groom and bride to experience joy.

Still, how can one be expected to ignore that which is clearly visible? The *Meshech Chochmah* provides a remarkable answer.

The Torah states, "And the *kohein* will see the blemish. . .and the *kohein* will see him" (*Vayikra* 13:3). First the *kohein* must inspect the blemish objectively and determine if it is the spiritual disease of *tzaraas*. Then he must look at the person and, if the situation warrants it, ignore the blemish. First the *kohein* sees the blemish, then the *kohein* sees *him*. If he is deserving, as a *chassan* is, the *kohein* does not announce the *tzaraas*.

The same criterion applies to the *chassan* and *kallah*. Of course they will see minor imperfections, but they must look at the total person. If each of them has all the positive features they seek in a spouse, then they must ignore any shortcomings discovered after the wedding. This lesson is essential not only for the week of *sheva berachos* but for the entire duration of a marriage.

My dear *chassan* and *kallah,* as we celebrate during a period of mourning, as we rejoice over a new *bayis beYisrael* at a time that recalls *Churban Habayis*, we hope that you will be blessed with *shalom bayis*. And we pray that all of us will overlook each other's faults and thereby merit the rebuilding of the ultimate *bayis,* the *Beis Hamikdash,* soon in our time.

Sefer Devarim

Rabbi Max Schreier

פרשת דברים
Parshas Devarim

BEFORE ENTERING THE HOLY LAND, the Jewish people are reproved by Moshe, who lists their sins in *Parshas Devarim*. His purpose is not to anger or shame the Jews but to motivate them to repent, to impress upon them one last time before his death that their destiny lies in obeying G-d and the commands of His Torah.

Rabbeinu Bechaye begins his commentary on this *parshah* with the words of Shlomo Hamelech: "Who rebukes a man will find grace afterward, more than who flatters" (*Mishlei* 28:23). The one who gives reproof is not popular, Rabbeinu Bechaye admits. "Rabbi Tarfon said, I wonder if their is anyone in the generation who accepts criticism. [Instead] he tells [his critic], 'Take the splinter out of your own teeth. . ..' Therefore the reprover is not accepted or liked by everyone, for some will hate him since he told them the truth of their actions. But the one who flatters is accepted and liked."

Rabbi Schreier is rav of the Avenue N Jewish Center in Brooklyn, New York.

Nevertheless, he concludes, the one who accepts criticism will find favor in G-d's eyes, "for words of criticism, when they are harsh, are what bring a person to success of the soul."

The best advice, therefore, is for one to be his own critic. Every person knows himself well enough to recognize his own faults, and if he is intellectually honest enough and objective enough, he will have the strength to admit them and work on improving his condition.

Never is there a better time for this sort of soul-searching and introspection than before one's wedding. Our Jewish tradition has passed along a variety of laws and customs to encourage this behavior. The *chassan* is called to the Torah on the Shabbos before his wedding. Being thrust into the spotlight, placed at the center of attention, he has the opportunity to reflect on his role in and his responsibility to the Jewish community.

On their wedding day, the couple observe a personal day of judgement and attonement. They fast; they say the Yom Kippur *viduy* prayer, confessing their sins before G-d; they go to the *mikvah* for ritual purification. Under the *chuppah,* the *chassan* wears a white *kittel* and the *kallah* wears a white gown. All these traditions serve to purify the couple, to focus their thoughts on the sanctity of their union and to bring them closer to G-d and Divine service.

The Divinity of the marriage union is noted in the last of the *sheva berachos*, which praises G-d, "Who created joy and gladness." This blessing purposely employs the word, *bara*, created, rather than the word, *yatzar*, formed. For while the distinction between the two words seems negligible, they have vastly different connotations.

Beriah is creating something new, something from nothing — *ex nihilo*. *Yetzirah*, on the other hand, is forming something from something else, something already in existence. The two terms are different not in degree but in kind: While man is capable of *yetzirah*, manufacturing new goods from raw materials, only G-d is capable of *beriah*, creating an entirely new entity.

Beriah is, therefore, the appropriate word for this *berachah*, enlightening us as to the nature of happiness. G-d creates joy and gladness, out of nothing at all. Too many people think they can stimulate happiness, that they can form it from something else; staking their happiness on possessions or events, they are left disappointed and unfulfilled. Happiness is so elusive when one tries to regiment it.

Instead, happiness arrives at unexpected moments. It comes, more often than not, out of nothing at all. *Ex nihilo*. When G-d sends His grace, that is when one can truly be happy. It is this Divine happiness, the kind emanating from G-d's holy throne, that our blessing bestows upon the new couple.

My dear *chassan* and *kallah,* as you begin a Jewish family, you re-assess yourselves and rededicate yourselves to the Jewish mission, bringing G-d in as a partner in your life together. Only He "Who creates joy and gladness" can grant you the happiness you both deserve. By beginning your lives afresh, highlighting the successes of your past and having cleansed yourselves of past faults, you guarantee yourselves G-d's grace. May your life and home enjoy all the variations of happiness listed in the blessing and enable you to be a herald of joy to your families and all of Israel.

Rabbi Ralph Pelcovitz

פרשת ואתחנן
Parshas Va'eschanan

ALTHOUGH WE ARE TAUGHT, "There is no sequence in the Torah," nonetheless, when a phrase or word appears several times in the Torah, there must be some significance to that particular order. The word I refer to is *ahavah* — love.

In *Sefer Bereishis*, one finds the word mentioned regarding Yitzchak and his wife, Rivkah (24:67), and again regarding Yaakov and his wife, Rachel (29:30). Love is mentioned again, between parents and children, when the Torah tells us of Rivkah's love for Yaakov (25:28) and Yaakov's love for Yosef (37:3). One can well understand that the emotion of love exists between man and wife, parent and child..

As one continues to study the other books of the *Chumash,* one finds that love is mentioned again in *Vayikra*, where the Jewish people are told to "Love your neighbor as yourself" (19:18). Proceeding to the fifth of the five books of the Torah, one finds what is probably the most

---

Rabbi Pelcovitz is rabbi emeritus of Congregation Knesseth Israel in Far Rockaway, New York.

sublime, and certainly the most sacred, of all loves: "And you shall love the L-rd, your G-d" (*Devarim* 6:5).

Considering that the Torah was given to the people of Israel as a guide to life and a primer of belief meant to provide a scale of priorities, would it not have been more logical for the Torah to first tell us to love G-d, even before we are told to love our fellow man? And since love is such a deep, profound emotion, shouldn't the Torah have commanded us to love G-d with all our heart and soul before speaking to us of the love between man and woman, and parent and child? Certainly there is nothing more noble or exalted than the commandment of loving G-d — even to the point of martyrdom.

Love is a deep-seated emotion — in many ways mysterious, irrational and even incomprehensible. Nonetheless, it is so real and powerful. How does it evolve in the human psyche. Even more important is the question: How is it learned? To love another beyond one's self must be learned. An infant loves himself reflexively, naturally, and this self-love remains for one's entire life. The expression used by our Sages, "A person is closest to himself," is understandable. This feeling is implanted in every human being, if only for the purpose of self-preservation.

But as one grows and matures, one learns to go beyond the self and interact with others. Nonetheless, the concept of love and concern for another is ephemeral and, to a child, non-concrete. How much more so is this true of G-d. All this is unreal to a child and must, therefore, be learned slowly, by doing *mitzvos* and through life's experiences.

There is a wise saying: "I hear and I forget. I see and I remember. I do and I understand." This is certainly true of the emotion of love, and a child must be exposed to it and learn it through relationships that are established between himself and his parents, family and friends.

The true meaning of love, however, is not understood until one marries. It is this that the Torah subtly teaches when it first introduces the word *ahavah*, speaking of the feelings of a *chassan* for his *kallah* and a *kallah* for her *chassan*. True, the word is also used to describe the feeling parents have for their children. But it is the love of a husband for his wife and a wife for her husband which implants in a person the true meaning of this word. It is in this relationship between husband and wife that one learns to be considerate and giving and concerned for the welfare of another. Once the Torah tells us that man has the ability to love his wife, then this inner-oriented lesson of love can be transferred and become outer oriented, extending beyond one's family to the family of Man. That is why "Love your neighbor as yourself" appears in the Torah later. Because had we been give this *mitzvah* first, it would have been unrealistic to expect one to fulfill it, for where is the training ground and preparation?

How much more so is this true of *ahavas Hashem*. It would have been unrealistic and futile to command us to love G-d, Who we cannot see or hear, unless we first learn the lesson of love in our relationships with others, be they a spouse or fellow man. When we learn how to be sensitive to the needs of others and develop feelings of love toward a spouse and friends, we are better prepared to harness this powerful emotion of love and channel it into our relationship with the A-mighty. It is, therefore, most sensible and understandable that the sequence in the Torah is love for a spouse, followed by love for fellow man, and ultimately, love for Hashem.

The Torah recognizes our weakness and frailty as human beings and does not impose on us the commandment of *ahavas Hashem* until we have been educated and trained in the university of home, family and community.

My dear *chassan* and *kallah,* we tend to believe that when one marries, one has already learned to fulfill all the *mitzvos* of *ahavah*. But this is not necessarily so. What we celebrate when we rejoice with you is your new appreciation of *ahavah*, which grows out of your love for one another. This is why the celebration of a *sheva berachos* is not only a blessing for you, but carries with it the added dimension of *ahavah* — love the Torah way.

Rabbi Abner Weiss

פרשת עקב
Parshas Eikev

THE JEWISH PEOPLE'S ULTIMATE MOMENT of national shame, their worshipping of the Golden Calf, is recounted in *Parshas Eikev*. Their apostasy is astonishing. How was it possible that, immediately after their encounter with G-d at Sinai, an unprecedented event in human history, they could build an idol? What could possibly account for this lapse?

In order to grasp this tragedy, one must carefully read the text and analyze the Jews' behavior at Sinai. When the Jews were to receive the Ten Commandments, they were to hear them from G-d's own voice. But after G-d told them the first and second Commandments, they became frightened to the point that their souls momentarily left their bodies. The Midrash says, "You speak to us and we shall hear," they told Moshe. "Let not G-d speak to us lest we die" (*Shemos* 20:16). The Jewish nation gave up the opportunity to continue to hear G-d's command from G-d Himself.

This collective experience of the Jewish people is symbolic of the individual experience of every Jewish couple. Just as Sinai, the national

---

Rabbi Weiss is rav of the Beth Jacob Congregation in Beverly Hills, California.

marriage of the Jewish people and G-d, is the paramount event of Jewish history, so too a couple's wedding serves as the high point and foundation of their relationship. In marriage, the participants are transformed and inspired. Just as the national pact of the Jewish people with G-d was sealed at Sinai, binding them to G-d eternally, so too the love expressed and committed publicly under the *chuppah* by every couple comes with the expectation that it will last forever.

Sadly though, this is increasingly not the case, even in our own Torah communities. The stars that once sparkled in the eyes of many couples dim. Hopes dissipate and commitments are broken. This downturn resembles the very one sustained nationally by the Jewish people, who, after preparing for three days to encounter G-d, flinch when the moment is upon them. They hear one commandment, two commandments, but no more from the mouth of G-d. "The nation stood at a distance and Moshe approached the thick darkness where G-d was" (20:18). The Jews distanced themselves from their Divine protector, and what happened next? Forty days later Moshe found them dancing around the Golden Calf.

Too many couples relive the reluctance of their ancestors. Instead of communicating with each other, they drift apart. Rather than sharing with each other their deepest concerns, they are paralyzed by fears and insecurities, terrified that honesty will damage their fragile relation-ships. As time passes, where they had once hoped to see light and inspiration, they perceive a thick darkness. Alienated and vulnerable, they seek salvation in other relationships.

Happily, though, this lamentable process is avoidable when one recognizes that the thick darkness only appears to be impenetrable from a distance. "Moshe approached the thick darkness where G-d was." Then the barrier lifted and he was enveloped in clouds of glory.

At Sinai, Moshe reassured the Jewish people. "Fear not," he told them, "for G-d has come to test you so that His fear should be upon your faces in order that you shall not sin." Fear of G-d means more than just being afraid; it includes awe, a recognition of G-d's power and control in this world. When a Jew is conscious of that power, when he feels that awe, he can not sin.

"What does G-d ask of you but to fear Him," Moshe asks the Jewish people in *Parshas Eikev*, "to go in all His ways, to love Him, and to serve the L-rd, your G-d, with all your heart and with all your soul" (*Devarim* 10:12). Once fear of G-d is in its proper place, all else follows logically. Nevertheless, "Is fear of Heaven such a simple thing?" the Talmud wants to know. "Yes. For Moshe it is a simple thing" (*Berachos* 33b). Moshe, who spoke with G-d face to face, who was personally devoted to G-d's every word, clearly comprehended G-d's glory.

To a couple, too, one can ask, "Is success in marriage such a simple thing?" And one can answer yes — if husband and wife are like Moshe, if they speak with each other face to face and are personally devoted to each other's every word. Then all else will follow logically.

Only when husband and wife stand far apart from each other do the barriers between them seem impervious. Only when they feel too vulnerable to chance an honest encounter with each other is communication impossible. They need to overcome those fears and anxieties. They must recognize that all love entails risk — risk of rejection, risk of abandonment, risk of loss — but they also must recognize that love is rewarding enough to justify the risk.

My dear *chassan* and *kallah*, our prayer for you is that you take upon yourselves the risks of loving; that you communicate clearly and honestly; that you never stand apart from each other, and that you ascend the mountain of G-d together and forge a path through the illusory darkness into genuine light.

Rabbi Binyamin Walfish

פרשת ראה
Parshas Re'eih

A S A *CHASSAN* AND *KALLAH* BEGIN their life together, they embark on an exciting journey that will add dimensions to their lives which could not have been anticipated. It is a journey that can be both joyful and rewarding, but one that is also fraught with certain dangers that need to be avoided as well as problems that need to be solved. Dealing with these challenges requires devotion to each other and to their family.

Parshas Re'eih begins with a simple declaration by G-d, "See that I place before you today blessing and curse" (*Devarim* 11:26). The Midrash tells the story of a king who made a great feast and invited many guests, including his best friend. When the food was served, the king told his friend to serve himself first, but the guest, not sure what to choose, paused. So the king guided his hand to the best serving.

G-d, too, asks His people to choose between blessing, observance of His Torah and *mitzvos,* and curse, rejection of His path. The Jewish

Rabbi Walfish was executive vice president of the Rabbinical Council of America and is now executive president of Otzar Haposkim in Jerusalem.

nation is then guided by the Divine hand of G-d to choose observance of Torah and its concomitant blessing. The Jewish people are presented with a way of life, a set of commandments to observe and to perform. These *mitzvos* bring joy and fulfillment to one's life. Not observing these *mitzvos,* departing from observance of Torah, going astray from the word of G-d brings trouble and pain.

What is the way of blessing? The *parshah* outlines the will of G-d, detailing many of the basic *mitzvos* of Judaism, including the laws of *kashrus,* charity and the holidays. These *mitzvos* cover the spectrum of the Jewish experience. The ritual *mitzvos* that concern a Jew's relationship with G-d, which appear to be without rationale except for the fact that they are G-d's will; and *mitzvos* that concern one's relationship to his fellow Jew, laws of ethics and morality, which are the foundation of any society. Thus, *Parshas Re'eih*, which speaks of these two aspects of Torah law — *bein adam laMakom* and *bein adam lachaveiro* — represents a microcosm of the Jewish mission.

With the Torah delineating these responsibilities, it seems that the choice would be clear. But it is not that simple. In practice, the line between blessing and curse is often blurred. To illustrate this, the Midrash contrasts two similar incidents in the Torah that occurred to great men, Adam and Avraham. Adam was offered fruit from the Tree of Knowledge by his wife, Chavah, and he listened to her and ate it. Consequently, the two were punished and driven from the Garden of Eden.

Avraham also listened to his wife, Sarah, when she told him to banish Hagar and her son, Yishmael, from his home. Consequently, he was able to raise his second son, Yitzchak, in a pristine environment, free from the ruinous influence of Yishmael.

Both Adam and Avraham were faced with dilemmas. Both chose to follow the advice of their wives. Yet the results of their actions were strikingly different. One was punished, the other blessed. What accounts for that difference?

In the case of Adam, G-d had already decreed that the Tree of Knowledge was off limits. He and Chavah were not to eat from it. But Adam defied G-d's will and ate. Not so Avraham, who was told by G-d, "All that Sarah tells you, listen to her" (*Bereishis* 21:12). Each of them had a responsibility to listen to his wife — but not when her advice clashed with G-d's command.

This is the lesson that must be learned by all married couples: Listen to each other, discuss every decision with each other. But remember that all resolutions must reflect the will of G-d.

My dear *chassan* and *kallah,* set before you today is this opportunity for *berachah*, the opportunity to bring G-d's Torah into your home and with it success and happiness into your lives. We know the families you come from, families in which Torah and *mitzvos* are emphasized and followed vigorously, families in which all members' actions reflect the will of G-d. We are therefore confident that you will follow in their footsteps and continue along their path in order to build your holy home in our nation upon a foundation of blessing.

Rabbi Herschel Billet

פרשת שופטים
Parshas Shoftim

HE WORD *MILCHAMAH* REFERS not only to war waged between nations, but also to the internal battles one faces when struggling with the challenges of life. Many of the sections of the Torah that discuss war in a military sense can also be applied allegorically to life's struggles.

Parshas Shoftim, for example. The *parshah* contains the procedure the Jewish people were to follow before going on to the battlefield to engage their enemies. G-d commands the *kohein* to address the soldiers first. "Do not lose heart," the *kohein* tells them. "Do not be afraid, do not be confounded, do not be broken because of them — for the L-rd is your G-d, Who walks with you to fight for you against your enemies, to save you" (*Devarim* 20:3-4).

His message can be applied to a newly married couple as well. As they confront a new life together, a Jewish couple must see themselves as warriors in G-d's army, struggling for the continuance of the Jewish people. A Jewish family comprises three partners: husband, wife and

---

Rabbi Billet is rav of the Young Israel of Woodmere, New York.

G-d. G-d's incorporation into the family structure should serve as a source of strength and confidence for every married couple. Do not lose heart, do not be confounded, because throughout the challenges of life G-d is your partner and He will always be there to assist you through the hard times.

Next, the Torah orders certain people off the battlefield. Due to their circumstances, the Ramban explains, these men would be distracted from the rigors of battle and would be likely to flee. They include those who had built houses but did not yet settle into them; those who had planted vineyards but did not yet enjoy their fruits; and those who were engaged to be married but did not yet do so.

These exemptions from military service provide crucial information as to what requires one's undivided attention — so much so that matters of national security have to take a back seat to them. What is the significance of these responsibilities that they take priority?

First, the home. The Talmud expounds upon the words of the verse. "The man who built a new house" (20:5) is exempted not only for having built a house *per se*, but also for other significant structures he may have built which require his attention, including silos for grain and stables for cattle (*Sotah* 43a). The inclusion of these is eye-opening. Husband and wife must take seriously their roles as builders, not merely as builders of the structure of a house, but as builders of all that is necessary to insure that that house is settled properly, that their house is turned into a home.

Second, the vineyard. The Torah finds symbolism in the vineyard. "For the vineyard of the L-rd of Hosts is the house of Israel," the prophet declares (*Yeshayahu* 5:7). Likewise, after the Temple was destroyed and the Sanhedrin relocated to the city of Yavneh, the body was referred to as *Kerem Beyavneh*, a Vineyard in Yavneh. It was so called, Rashi explains, because the members of the Sanhedrin sat in rows, resembling the arrangement of rows in a vineyard (*Berachos* 63b).

But one can also see the term referring to something more than the Sanhedrin's physical arrangement; the vineyard represents the spiritual infrastructure of the Jewish people, the same spiritual infrastructure necessary for a successful marriage. Just as the Jewish people, the spiritual light to the nations of the world, and just as the Sanhedrin, the spiritual guiders of the Jewish people, are called vineyards, so too a new couple must plant their own vineyard, setting down the roots of spirituality within their union.

Third, the union itself. Marriage is a lifelong commitment. "The Torah taught the proper way," teaches the Talmud, "that a person should build a house and plant a vineyard, and afterward marry a woman" (*Sotah* 44a). The Maharsha qualifies this statement: "One who is able should follow this order, marrying a woman last," but one who is unable to do so is not prohibited from marrying (*Torah Temimah*). Still, the Rambam, referring to this prescription, describes as fools those who would marry before properly preparing for the responsibilities of marriage. *Chassan* and *kallah* bind their lives and futures together — not a simple act, but one that requires a concentrated effort of patience and understanding and the unremitting desire to make things work despite the travails.

My dear *chassan* and *kallah*, the two of you are worthy to serve as warriors among the ranks of *Klal Yisrael*. You have the education and the preparation to be master builders. You have signaled your preparedness to make sacrifices for others and for your nation. You have witnessed the shining examples of your families who serve as models for your family. You have seen firsthand what distinguishes a Jewish home from other homes, and what connects one's home to Jewish history and Jewish destiny. May you be a source of light and fulfillment for each other and for your families, and may G-d bless your home with children who will be a source of joy and pleasure to you and who will insure the continuity of our people.

Rabbi Yaacov Haber

פרשת שופטים

פרשת שופטים
Parshas Shoftim

BEFORE THEIR MARRIAGE, a *chassan* and *kallah* spend large amounts of time discussing their future. Together they stand on the threshold of one of life's greatest endeavors and challenges. Upon entering a marriage they make a lifetime commitment to a relationship, to parenthood, to creating a home. They pledge devotion to each other, discuss practical ways to build a home of charity and peace, and resolve to "always be there" for their children.

Then they get married and something happens. Reality sets in. The demands of the moment cloud their view of the big picture. The nitty-gritty of life overwhelms them and they find themselves asking, "What happened to this marriage, this home, these children? Where did I go wrong?"

The conflict between idealism and reality is as old as the ancient kings of Israel, who provide a telling image in *Parshas* Shoftim.

G-d commands the king of Israel to carry a *Sefer Torah* with him wherever he goes. The nation's leader, says G-d, can never be seen

---

Rabbi Haber is director of Jewish education at the Orthodox Union.

without the Torah close to his heart. When he convenes his ministry and meets with his officers, he must have his Torah with him. As he marches onto the battlefield, he must carry his Torah. Even when he strolls through the marketplace, the king must never be separated from his Torah.

But that's not all.

The king of Israel is commanded to keep a second *Sefer Torah* locked away in his treasury, never to be seen with him. A curious *halachah*? No. A fitting solution to a practical problem. Since the king carries his Torah everywhere, the air and elements it is exposed to take their toll. Gradually, letters crack, fade, fall off. So slow is this process that the king may not realize that the Torah he is carrying is not the same one he set out with at the start of his reign.

G-d tells the king, therefore, Don't rely on this Torah alone. Keep a pristine copy in the treasury, not to be exposed to the winds and wars of life. Let its characters remain intact. While your cradled Torah fades and cracks, your treasured Torah will stay sharp and flawless.

But from time to time, the king is told, bring your public Torah into your inner chambers. Open both and place them side by side on a table. Then, don't just compare them, correct them. Review and renew your standards. Do not allow the faded Torah to become the standard for you and your people.

This check and correct process applies to us today as well. Every one of us fashions a set of principles, a personal *Sefer Torah,* by which to live, unbiased and untainted by the winds and wars of life. But as we go through life, these principles begin to fade, crack and fall apart.

So the Torah gives us good advice: Retreat to your inner chambers for reflection. Compare and correct. Life is full of challenges and pitfalls and we're only human. But our original standard is Divine and is to be treasured and called upon for review and renewal, enabling us to go out once again and face life with the clarity of our youth.

My dear *chassan* and *kallah,* the kabbalists teach that first thoughts are holy. Inscribe those idealistic thoughts not on parchment but on your hearts. Keep your character intact by recording those initial dreams and goals. Always refer to them, for in them lies the secret to G-dliness and growth.

Rabbi Aaron J. Fink

פרשת כי תצא
Parshas Ki Seitzei

A YIDDISHE WEDDING AND *SHEVA BERACHOS* represent a special opportunity for rejoicing. Marriage, the joining of a new couple as life partners setting out to build their own Jewish home and to establish another branch on the tree of Jewish continuity, is certainly a cause for celebration. But in order for that celebration to last beyond the wedding day, one must know what qualities need to be incorporated into the marriage itself.

In *Parshas Ki Seitzei*, the Torah describes, through two *mitzvos,* the priorities critical to successful Jewish living. One is studied and debated thoroughly, scrutinized for its philosophical as well as its legal ramifications. The other is less known and its message is unfortunately overlooked. Taken together, they provide a contrast that brings into focus the Torah's view of marriage and family.

The *parshah* begins with the dilemma of a soldier who has gone to war and won. He emerges from his victory with a maiden he has captured in the heat of the battle and for whom he yearns. The Torah

---

Rabbi Fink is principal of Yeshivat Hadar Avraham Tzvi in Monsey, New York.

defines the conditions and procedures by which this type of relationship may be consummated. This allowance seems astounding, and, in fact, the Talmud declares that, in allowing this union to take place, the Torah is making an accommodation to man's evil impulse (*Kiddushin* 21b). While the Torah requires that the soldier be discouraged from taking her, he is allowed to do so if he insists. The Torah understands human nature and prefers, in this case, to permit an act rather than forbid it and invite transgression.

Nevertheless, the Talmud's harsh classification of this union results from its resting upon underpinnings of temptation and desire created in the heat of the moment, rather than upon love and trust built over time. The soldier's feelings for her are an infatuation, a fantasy, a fling, which sadly, yet aptly, reflects the current trend in our society, "the land of the free." In response, the Torah demands an active effort on his part to eliminate this superficial attraction before allowing him to begin living with this woman.

It is no coincidence that the subsequent topics addressed in this *parshah* are the fates of the unloved wife and the rebellious child. These scenarios serve as warnings to those who would indulge in such a shallow lifestyle. "If he marries her, he will hate her in the end," Rashi says, "and the result will be that she gives birth to a rebellious son." The Torah warns that physical beauty is only skin-deep; much more is required in order to achieve sanctity in marriage and to perpetuate the eternity of Israel.

That sanctity is manifested many verses later in the *parshah* in the *mitzvah* that not only exempts but prohibits a newlywed from fighting in the army. Before one is allowed to go out and fight for his people, he must first establish himself on the home front — and this takes time. New relationships need nurturing. They cannot be disturbed. The obligations a Jew has to his people is secondary to the budding commitment a husband must have to his wife, and she to him.

The couple is commanded to dedicate their first year of married life to each other, to rejoicing together. "He shall be available at home for one year and make his wife happy" (*Devarim* 24:5). In order to build marital harmony, husband and wife must set aside other obligations and invest time in their relationship. The Torah demands that time, one's most precious commodity, be reserved for those held dear. "For a full year from the moment he married her," the *Sefer Hachinuch* writes, the husband will devote himself to his wife "in order to become accustomed to her and grow fond of her." Marital love, says the Torah, requries time to ripen. Only with time do emotional and spiritual interdependence flourish.

My dear *chassan* and *kallah,* always make time to share the precious moments of life with each other. All your friends and family members know that you will dedicate yourselves to the Jewish mission, but first you start at home. Celebrate, rejoice with each other. It is the only way to insure that the great affection you have for each other at this time, the dawn of your relationship, will evolve into an everlasting love that will carry you forth to a hundred and twenty healthy and happy years together.

Rabbi Simcha Krauss

פרשת כי תבוא
Parshas Ki Savo

I N PARSHAS KI SAVO, G-D THREATENS the Jewish people with 98 curses, warning them never to deviate from the principles of His Torah. With so many curses looming over them, the Jews were struck with terror. How could they succeed? To counteract this threat, the *Chiddushei Harim* notes, a couple is given the opportunity, through the *sheva berachos*, for 98 blessings. When the seven blessings of *sheva berachos* are repeated at each of two daily meals during the first week of marriage, the total number of blessings comes to 98.

These blessings are meant to carry the newlyweds through life. Jews live in a world that is often unfriendly and even hostile. How shall they protect themselves? With all the curses that are piled upon them from the outside, how shall they create an island of security and sanctity, a land of loyal and dedicated Jewish homes which tries to live up to the blessings contained in the *sheva berachos*?

The key to creating such a home can be summed up in the wisdom of Reb Mendel of Kotzk. "Where can you find G-d?" he would ask.

Rabbi Krauss is rav of the Young Israel of Hillcrest in Queens, New York.

"Wherever you let him in." The first step toward success is to invite G-d in.

The *mitzvah,* described in *Parshas Ki Savo*, to bring to the Temple one's *bikurim*, one's first fruits, illustrates how one brings G-d into his home. A Jew is commanded to devote not only the first but also the choicest fruits of his labors to G-d. In doing so, he demonstrates the quality and urgency of his commitment to G-d. Today, in the absence of a Temple, one has to search for alternatives to prove this commitment.

My dear *chassan* and *kallah,* your mutual ambitions demonstrate your devotion to G-d and to His Torah. Your determination to dedicate your educations and your talents to serving the Jewish people are the *bikurim* that you offer. In doing so, you establish a miniature Temple and insure that only blessings will emanate from your home.

Ari Dov Ganchrow

פרשת כי תבוא
Parshas Ki Savo

THE *PARSHAH* OF *KI SAVO* BEGINS with a description of an act of thanksgiving, a beautiful ceremony in tribute to Hashem. The *mitzvah* of *bikurim* — the bringing of the first fruits to the Temple — was initiated only after Eretz Yisrael was captured and divided. The *mitzvah* expresses a Jew's appreciation of owning land and benefiting from its produce, of acquiring material wealth in accordance with the instructions of Hashem. This national institution of *bikurim* became a joyous celebration lasting through the summer months, from Shavuos to Sukkos.

The fruits that were brought were the finest, most select of the seven special species. How was the fruit chosen? The owner would go to his orchard, see fruit ripening, tie a ribbon around each and declare "*Harei eilu bikurim* — These are the first fruits." He would then put the fruit in a basket, bring it to the Temple and present it to the *kohein,* who placed it by the altar.

The mishnah in *Bikurim* (3:2-4) outlines the pomp and ceremony of the procession to Jerusalem. It was led by an ox whose horns were

Ari Ganchrow is an attorney living in Englewood, New Jersey.

bedecked with gold. (Rabbi Moshe Tendler points out that an ox was chosen to lead the parade to show appreciation for its plowing, which contributed to a successful crop.) The leader would announce, "Rise and we shall go up to Zion, to the L-rd our G-d" (*Yirmiyahu* 31:5), and as they travelled they chanted, "I was glad when they told me, Let us go to the house of G-d" (*Tehillim* 122:1).

As they approached Jerusalem they sent messengers ahead to announce their arrival and the city's residents would come out to welcome them. The *bikurim* were brought in not singly but in large groups to fulfill the verse, "*Berav am hadras melech* — In a multitude is the glory of the king" (*Mishlei* 14:28).

In his commentary, the *Sefas Emes* notes that everything G-d created serves to glorify him. In each 24-hour cycle we pray three times, acknowledging that nothing exists through its own might. Every season, every period and cycle is a temporary gift from G-d, whose power over nature is clear to us. These first fruits represent a climax, a symbol of the joy and gratitude of man to the One Above Who granted a harvest for the year. These are indeed first fruits, new and beautiful, not a continuation of last year's crop. For this we express our gratitude.

Unlike animal sacrifices, which were allowed, for a time, to be offered on private altars, the *bikurim* ceremony is exclusively a public one, taking place only in Shiloh, where the Tabernacle stood before the Temple was built, and later in the Temple itself in Jerusalem. *Bikurim* are a public not a private act of thanksgiving, a *mitzvah* irradiated with beauty to emphasize its deep significance and its message of the G-d-given freshness of life.

The celebration of a marriage is not simply a personal party but also a means of expressing thanks to Hashem who brought this couple to this day, who gave them the privilege to grow up as Torah Jews in a Torah society. Just as a Jew goes into the field and proclaims, "*Harei eilu bikurim,*" when the fruit is not yet completely ripe, so too the young couple pledge themselves, at the dawn of their development, to divine service. They make not a wish but a commitment.

My dear *chassan* and *kallah,* may you work together for *Klal Yisrael* to bring our people closer to Hashem so that we can all proclaim once again, "Rise and we shall go up to Zion, to the L-rd our G-d."

Rabbi Elazar R. Muskin

פרשת נצבים־וילך
Parshas Nitzavim-Vayeilech

N*ETZAVIM* AND *VAYEILECH* are the two *parshios* that are always read either on the Shabbos that precedes Rosh Hashanah or on the one that follows it. That they occupy this exclusive spot on the Jewish calendar, at the start of a new year, is informative and bodes well for a *chassan* and *kallah* as they mark the beginning of their life together.

In the first verse of *Parshas Vayeilech*, the Torah records that on the last day of his life, "Moshe went out and spoke these words to all of Israel" (*Devarim* 31:1). What does the Torah mean "Moshe went'? Where exactly did he go? Whom did he have to visit during his last precious hours on earth?

The Ramban explains that Moshe went to visit the twelve tribes, to personally deliver to each a copy of the Torah and to announce to each G-d's selection of Yehoshua as his successor to the mantle of Jewish leadership. A fine explanation, but questions remain. Why did Moshe feel compelled to visit each tribe individually? Could he not have

---

Rabbi Muskin is rav of the Young Israel of Century City in Los Angeles, California.

simply gathered all the Jews together as he had done many times before?

Obviously, Moshe could have called on all of Israel to assemble together, but he recognized that no matter how powerful his words would be and no matter how dramatic the moment, a public address has limited appeal and restricted influence. While many speakers enjoy a larger audience, for it enhances their egos, the message they impart is inherently limited by the size of the group to whom it is delivered. Why? Because in a crowd, no one feels personally bound by the message. Everyone assumes that the speaker is addressing someone else. When someone lectures a group about its behavior, each person in the audience fools himself into thinking that his neighbor, not he, is the one who needs to be chastised.

Moshe Rabbeinu would not cater to this rationalizing. On the day of his death, he met with the tribes individually in the hope they would recognize that his message was for them, not just others. Moshe understood the importance of personal communication and direct contact. His words took on extra power because they were addressed to each member personally; no one was allowed to be lost in the crowd.

By taking his message down to a more personal level, Moshe also underscored the importance of each individual in the community and each individual's efforts for the community. Every Jew must contribute his or her unique talents to the Jewish people. And each one is necessary; no one can fill another's place or do the other's job.

This dual lesson, which Moshe keenly demonstrated, should have an impact on every *chassan* and *kallah*. First, that communication is a vital component of a healthy marriage. And, once a healthy marriage is established, that every family and every family member has the responsibility to find a public role within the Jewish nation. Each couple, each person, has a unique contribution to make; they should never think their involvement is unimportant or that they are replaceable.

The Talmud records the prayer of Rabbi Elazar: "May it be Your will, L-rd our G-d, that in our lot dwell love, brotherhood, peace and friendship; that you increase the disciples in our borders; make our end succeed with prospect and hope; place our share in the Garden of Eden; provide us with a good friend and a good inclination in your world that we may rise and find the desire of our heart to revere your name; and may satisfaction of our souls come before you for good" (*Berachos* 16b).

The Maharsha comments that this blessing alludes to marital bliss. It begins with a prayer for the same four qualities found in the last blessing of *sheva berachos*: love, brotherhood, peace and friendship. In addition, the prayer contains requests to promote the welfare of the community. A Jewish couple must not only worry about themselves, but must be concerned with the promotion of Torah scholarship and good neighbors. Marital bliss is coupled with responsibility for the community. When both these elements exist in a marriage, all other blessings will follow.

My dear *chassan* and *kallah,* Rav Elazar teaches that you do not need many friends, only one good friend — your spouse, with whom you can share all of your dreams and concerns. May it be G-d's will that you find lasting happiness with each other and that you are blessed with both spiritual and material blessings so that you may participate in the growth and development of the community, and benefit from it as well.

Rabbi Chaim Wasserman

פרשת האזינו
Parshas Haazinu

O

NE OF THE STRONGEST INDICATIONS to people that they have found their lifelong mate is free-flowing lines of communication. Each yearns to hear from the other, waiting impatiently for the phone to ring and, when it does, talking for hours on end (check your phone bills). This is a reliable litmus test, as Shlomo Hamelech writes in *Shir Hashirim*, "Let me hear your voice for it is pleasant" (2:14). Once in love, two people want to hear from each other endlessly.

At the start of their marriage, each partner hopes these feelings will last a lifetime. But unfortunately, the desire to "let me hear your voice" dissipates. Over time, rather than holding on to each word, people tend, tragically, to ignore what the other is saying regardless of its importance. Why does this change occur? How can it be avoided? How does a couple preserve these lines of communication while they are still open?

Consider three basic guidelines for artful listening.

First, listening is an act in which one's humanity is expressed. "Of all the things that human beings do," writes Mortimer Adler, "conversing

---

Rabbi Wasserman is rav of the Young Israel of Passaic-Clifton, New Jersey.

with one another is the most characteristically human. It may be in the long run the only human activity the performance of which will ultimately preserve the radical distinction between humans and brutes and between men and machines."

Many centuries before, Onkelus interpreted the verse that describes the creation of man: "*Vayehi ha'adam lenefesh chayah*" (*Bereishis* 2:7). These words are usually understood to mean that after G-d breathed life into man, "man became a living soul." But Onkelus renders the phrase, "It was in man as a speaking spirit." It is man's power of speech that defines him, setting him apart from the other creations.

"Shared thoughts and feelings," Adler continues, "understood agreements and disagreements, make humans the only animals that genuinely commune with one another. Even though they signal their emotions or impulses to one another, other animals remain shut out from each other. They do not commune with one another when they communicate. The human community would not exist without such communion, which would not exist without human conversation."

Successful human conversation requires two parties; the greatest frustration is to speak when no one is listening. When the Jews did not observe the Torah, G-d Himself said, "I called and no one answered" (*Yeshayahu* 50:2). When a man and a woman respond to each other, love and concern are manifested.

Second, active listening is always an exercise in discovery and learning. Conversation between a married couple needs to be properly understood.

"I'm cold," she says.

"I'll turn up the heat," he tells her. "But I don't feel chilly. Are you feeling all right?"

She bursts into tears. He remains confused. "What did I say? I was trying to be helpful."

He does not understand that when his wife says, "I'm cold," she means "I need closeness and reassurance."

In another instance, a couple fights over the garbage. "Take it out," she demands. "I can't stand the sight of it."

"But the garbage bag is barely half-full," he protests. "Nothing in it smells bad. Why take it out?"

They argue. Both are confused and angry. What the husband does not know is that at the bottom of the garbage is a pot full of burned Swedish meatballs, which his wife tried to make for the first time just for him. She even used his mother's recipe. The garbage testifies to her failure and she wants it out of sight.

These are two examples of how every act of listening entails more than hearing what is on the surface. Every conversation contains ideas and perspectives that need unearthing. The ability to consistently discover new ways of looking at things is central to a marriage and to the entire human experience.

Third, daily practice of the art of listening is an important feature in guaranteeing your mutual happiness and serenity in life amid the inevitable pressure and stress. The one dominant feature among couples whose marriages have lasted decades is effective communication. Certainly there were disagreements and even fights along the way. But by listening to each other, by working things out with communication, these couples did not allow their disagreements to degenerate into discord and then unbridgeable dissension.

My dear *chassan* and *kallah,* in *Parshas Haazinu*, Moshe asks heaven and earth to listen and attest to his final message. For as long as G-d grants the two of you life together, I wish that you bless each other with the gift of *haazinu*, the gift of listening and understanding each other. In this way, your feelings of love for each other and your commitment to each other will be nurtured and will insure that your life together will be happy and complete.

Rabbi Marvin E. Jacob

פרשת וזאת הברכה
Parshas Vezos Haberachah

V EZOS HABERACHAH IS THE ONLY PARSHAH in the Torah which is not read on any specific Shabbos. It is reserved for reading on Simchas Torah. *Vezos Haberachah* will therefore rarely be the subject of a *sheva berachos* sermon, since it is impermissible to make weddings on *Yom Tov* or *Chol Hamo'eid,* and most *poskim* prohibit making weddings during the *aseres yemei teshuvah*, the ten days of penitence. For these reasons, this sermon has been prepared so that it is applicable to other *parshios* as well.

In *Vezos Haberachah*, we again read about the passing of Moshe Rabbeinu after forty years of leadership of *Klal Yisrael.* In connection with his passing, the Torah emphasizes that he was the greatest of all of the Jewish prophets. Hashem communicated with him face to face. All of the other prophets received their prophecies while in a catatonic trance. In addition, the Torah makes clear that Moshe was the humblest of all men (*Bamidbar* 12:3).

Rabbi Jacob is a practicing attorney in New York City.

Similarly, in *Tehillim* (8:6), David Hamelech indicates that Moshe's erudition in Torah surpassed that of any other Jewish scholar. In that regard, he achieved a level somewhat less than that of the angels. As the Talmud states, Moshe mastered 49 of the fifty gates of understanding (*Rosh Hashanah* 21b). Also, the kabbalists note that when Moshe ascended Mount Nebo, as he was about to depart this world, he achieved mastery of the fiftieth gate as well. Thus, even before his death, Moshe passed from the finite into the domain of the infinite. In sum, Moshe's achievements were unparalleled in the areas of Torah scholarship, prophecy and humility.

Somewhat more obscure, however, are two other characteristics of Moshe's personality which made him the greatest of all Jewish leaders — his boundless love of *Klal Yisrael* and his selfless giving. For example, as the Jewish people stood on the brink of extinction, as a result of the sin of the Golden Calf, his statement, "Erase me from Your book" (*Shemos* 32:32), was not merely an offer to be deleted from G-d's Torah. As the Midrash explains, by those three words Moshe meant: Let Moshe and a thousand like him perish, but let no harm come to a single Jew (*Tanchuma*, *Beha'alosecha* 6). What a noble expression of love and self-sacrifice!

Neither did Moshe seek any compensation from the Jewish people for his many years of toil on their behalf. As he pointed out to *Klal Yisrael*, "I did not seek use of even a single donkey" (*Bamidbar* 16:15). And, as Rashi explains, even when it was necessary to transport his wife and sons from Midyan to Egypt, and under circumstances where he was entitled to the use of an animal by reason of his position as king, Moshe provided his own means of transportation. In fact, as the Talmud points out, Moshe's selfless giving was carefully crafted to avoid taking anything at all, even the use of a donkey, in return for his labors (*Megillah* 9a).

For these reasons, of the ten names by which Moshe was known, Hashem selected the name Moshe. As the Midrash relates, Moshe had ten names (*Vayikra Rabbah* 1:3). Thus, the Mirrer *rosh yeshiva,* Rav Chaim Shmulevitz, asks, why indeed did Hashem prefer the name Moshe over the others? He explains that a great deal of wisdom is necessary to give a person his true name. Although it would appear that the name Moshe was merely a description of the fact that Bisya,

Pharaoh's daughter, saved Moshe from drowning, Bisya's act was only possible through self-sacrifice, *mesiras nefesh*. She needed to defy her father's rigid decree in order to save Moshe's life, thereby imperiling her own. Since the life of Moshe was made possible only through an act of selfless giving and self-sacrifice, those characteristics irretrievably entered Moshe's body, soul and psyche.

Therein lies the formula, not only for great leadership, but also for *shalom bayis* and a happy marriage. *Chassan* and *kallah* must be imbued with love for each other and an attitude of selfless giving. Rav Eliyahu Eliezer Dessler, the *mashgiach* of the Ponevizer yeshiva, sums it up as follows: There are two attitudes in life — the "giving" attitude and the "taking" attitude. The power of selfless giving is the most elevated of all human characteristics. In fact, it is this power that the Torah refers to when it says that man was created in the image of G-d (*Bereishis* 1:26). On the other hand, taking is the egoistic urge to draw to oneself whatever comes into one's orbit, to get as much as one can for oneself in every situation and to give as little as possible in return. The attitude of taking is probably the source of most of the unhappiness and evil in this world.

Generally, love and giving develop together, especially in a happy marriage. By fulfilling each other's needs, man and wife become givers to each other and love often results from the giving itself. This love, in turn, engenders further giving, which intensifies the love each has for the other. Giving is therefore a dynamic and perpetuating process.

Accordingly, the best advice one can offer a *chassan* and *kallah* is: See that each of you always makes it your primary concern to give the other happiness; see that each of you maintains the striving to give selflessly to the other. Rest assured, the moment, G-d forbid, either departs from that attitude and begins making demands on the other, happiness is nearing its end.

In the *sheva berachos*, which are recited under the *chuppah* and during the seven days of rejoicing, the *chassan* and *kallah* are referred to as "beloved friends." Why is it necessary to modify the word "friend" with the word "beloved"? Isn't the word "friend" infused with the notion of love? The answer, as you may well understand from your own experience, is that friendships are often illusory. How often have you heard it said that "with friends like these, you don't need enemies"?

Indeed, that is why the word "friend" in the Hebrew language contains the same two letters that mean evil, or the very opposite of love. For friends may be temporary and have ulterior purposes. Only when the word "beloved" is added does it connote a friendship that is genuine; only when friendship is coupled with love can there be selfless giving rather than selfish taking.

As the Chassid Yaavetz points out in his commentary on *Pirkei Avos*, the words "friend" and "beloved" in the first mishnah of the sixth *perek* are meant to be read together. Citing the same phrase, "beloved friends," in the *sheva berachos*, he explains that when marriage is predicated upon the foundation of Torah, husband and wife can be described as beloved friends. Such a marriage properly focuses on the salient attitude of giving, rather than on the destructive attitude of taking.

May you together build a *bayis ne'eman beYisrael* based upon love and giving. May you be blessed with children who will carry forward our noble traditions and may your *shalom bayis* and other good deeds speed the coming of the *Moshiach* and the realization of the glorious destiny of the Jewish people. *Mazel tov*!

❧ Additional Divrei Torah for Sheva Berachos

Rabbi J. Simcha Cohen

Question: At the conclusion of *sheva berachos*, three persons customarily drink wine: the person who led *birkas hamazon* as well as the *chassan* and *kallah.* What is the procedure for drinking wine when *sheva berachos* take place at *shalosh seudos* in the late afternoon on Shabbos?

Response: A means of enhancing *birkas hamazon* is to hold a cup of wine (*kos shel berachah*) during the *birkas hamazon* and upon its conclusion to chant the *berachah*, "*hagafen*," prior to drinking of the wine. *Shalosh seudos* generally extends past sunset. Under normal circumstances one may not drink or eat food at such a late period of time on Shabbos. At issue is whether the person who held the cup of wine for *birkas hamazon* late Shabbos afternoon may, subsequent to *birkas hamazon*, recite the *berachah* over the wine and actually drink the wine at that period of time.

The *Magein Avraham* rules that one may drink the wine of a *kos shel berachah* even after *birkas hamazon*. Why? Because the wine relates to the meal. Just as a person could continue eating or drinking until *birkas*

Rabbi Cohen is rav of the Mizrachi Kehilla in Melbourne, Australia.

hamazon takes place, no matter how late it may be, for all food during the meal is permissible, so too is the wine of a *kos shel berachah* permissible, as it is considered part of the meal. There is a limitation, however, says the *Magein Avraham*. The person who drinks the wine must customarily do so after every *birkas hamazon*. The wine, then, becomes a part of the meal itself. If, however, the person who led *birkas hamazon* usually does not have a *kos shel berachah* after *birkas hamazon*, then he should not drink the wine after *shalosh seudos* (*Orach Chaim* 299:7).

The *Kuntras Acharon* of the *Taamai Minhagim* (993) notes that one Chassidic rebbe drank wine at *sheva berachos* on Shabbos afternoon and also gave the bride and groom to drink. His reason was the belief that the Tzaddik from Lublin drank wine every Shabbos after *birkas hamazon* of each meal. The implication is that if a person does not normally drink wine at *shalosh seudos*, then he should drink no wine at *sheva berachos* occurring at such a period of time.

Indeed, the general custom is to hold a cup of wine during the *birkas hamazon* of a regular *shalosh seudos* and not to recite a *"hagafen"* over it, but to subsequently use that wine for *havdalah*. Accordingly, maybe no one should drink any wine after the Shabbos afternoon *sheva berachos* meal.

Common custom, however, is to have the *chassan* and *kallah* drink the wine. My feeling is that this is based upon the halachic consideration of Rav Avraham Butchacha who, in two different commentaries, argues that drinking wine at *sheva berachos* is qualitatively different from drinking wine at a regular *shalosh seudos* on Shabbos.

His rationale is as follows:

At *sheva berachos*, the last *berachah* is chanted over wine. Should this blessing not be recited, then only six, not seven, *berachos* would be recited. Yet, seven blessings are mandated for a bride and groom. Accordingly, the wine should be drunk to eliminate problems with (Heaven forbid) reciting a blessing in vain (see *Aishel Avraham*, *mahadura tinyana*, *Orach Chaim* 22:7). The distinction is that on a regular Saturday afternoon one simply does not recite the wine blessing after *birkas hamazon* should the hour be late. Since *"hagafen"* is recited at *sheva berachos*, the wine should be drunk.

The author of the *Minchas Shabbos*, my paternal grandfather, cites (in his additive notes, *Shirurai Haminchah* 94:4) that Rav Avraham

Butchacha, in his commentary on *Even Ha'ezer* (62), a theory supports drinking wine at *sheva berachos* on Shabbos afternoon. Why? Because a person who regularly drinks wine after *birkas hamazon* is definitely permitted to drink the *kos shel berachah* after *shalosh seudos*. Since a *chassan* and *kallah* conclude each meal during the first week after their marriage with seven blessings, which include a blessing for wine, they are classified as people who normally drink wine after *birkas hamazon*.

[It is reputed that Rav Moshe Feinstein's position is that it is preferable for only the *chassan* and *kallah* to drink the wine after *shalosh seudos*, not the person who led the *birkas hamazon*. Rav Avraham Butchacha's logic may be the rationale for Rav Moshe's practice. Since the *chassan* and *kallah* regularly drank wine after the meal during their first week of marriage, they are certainly permitted to continue to drink the wine on Shabbos. The person who leads the *birkas hamazon*, however, does not have the same custom. He simply does not drink wine generally after a meal.

Indeed, at a recent *sheva berachos* on Shabbos afternoon, such was my custom. When I was honored to lead the *birkas hamazon*, I did not drink the wine but gave the *chassan* and *kallah* to drink. Moreover, to the extent that such wine is deemed potent for good tidings, it would be wrong to withhold such *mazel tov* from them.

It should be noted that the custom of Rav Yosef Zvi Dushinsky, former Chief Rabbi of Jerusalem, was to himself sip some wine and then give wine to the *chassan* and *kallah* (*Minhagei Maharitz*, 58).]

Rabbi Fabian Schonfeld

Sason VeSimcha

L OOKING AT THE TEXT OF THE BERACHAH, *"Asher bara sason vesimcha"*, it is difficult to understand why the blessing speaks of *sason* and *simcha*, joy and gladness, as being creations of the A-mighty. Hashem created men and women with the ability to be joyful and happy. How can those emotions be considered creations in their own right?

The answer may lie in the peculiar and particular way in which Jews celebrate happiness and joy. Before national secular holidays the local authorities predict the number of accidents and casualties brought on by the so-called spirit of the day. But no one has to forecast the number of casualties and accidents expected to take place during a Yom Tov or Purim. The explanation is simply that the way the Jewish people celebrate happiness and joy is totally different from the way in which others do.

Joy and happiness can be occasioned by many things, none of which have any kind of spirituality. The winning of a lottery or a promotion at

---

Rabbi Schonfeld is rav of the Young Israel of Kew Gardens Hills in Queens, New York.

work, which would certainly cause people to be happy, have no spiritual roots. Even births and weddings are celebrated by others without paying much heed to the spiritual significance of such an event.

When reciting *birkas hamazon* at a *sheva berachos* dinner, one refers to Hashem *"shehasimcha bemo'ano*, in Whose dwelling there is joy." *Sheva berachos* symbolize the kind of happiness and joy that was experienced at the wedding and is of spiritual and sacred dimension. That kind of joy and happiness is of Divine origin and, indeed, a creation of the A-mighty.

Rabbi Zalman Posner

Eloquent Silence

THE CUSTOM AT JEWISH WEDDINGS has the *chassan* saying, *"Harei at mekudeshes li"* under the *chupah,* while the *kallah* says nothing.

After the *chupah* friends congratulate the couple and their parents with a simple *"Mazel tov,"* to which the response will usually be a simple "Thank you."

"How does it feel to marry off a child?" they may ask.

"Wonderful." Hardly an adequate response to sum up the occasion.

Mazel tov. Thank you. That's about it. Why the sudden loss of speech?

Turn to a different time on the Jewish calendar: Rosh Hashanah. Its most memorable moment is the sounding of the shofar. No words, not even a melody. Just long blasts and short blasts.

What is the climax of the Rosh Hashanah prayers? Most would answer, *"Unesaneh tokef,"* a short prayer that asks simply, Who will live? And who, G-d forbid, will not?

The deeper the feeling, the fewer the words. The shofar blast is the sound of silence, the inarticulate cry of the heart, a sound higher than speech.

Rabbi Posner is rav of Congregation Sherith Israel in Nashville, Tennessee.

The parents of the happy couple are not terribly articulate on the evening of the wedding, but the feelings stirring in their hearts go far beyond anything words can convey. Their *simcha* can not be compressed into words.

Why does the *chassan* speak? Because he must declare his purpose before two witnesses that the ring he holds is for *kiddushin*, sanctification, dedication, marriage. Nine words declare this purpose; nothing else need be said. Any embellishment would diminish the moment.

And the *kallah*? This is the most sublime moment of her life, towering over any words a Shakespeare could compose.

My dear *chassan* and *kallah,* our blessings can be put into a few words. May Hashem grant you every *berachah*, all that you wish for yourselves, all your parents wish for you. May you rejoice always and may all Israel rejoice always with you.

Rabbi Shlomo Riskin

Creation

HE TORAH OPENS ON THE GRANDEST and loftiest scale possible — the creation of the world: heavens and earth, firmament, sun, moon, stars, and the planet itself. Each day we climb the ladder of creation until the sixth day when man appears.

But even after man's appearance, the epoch described seems remote, carried out of a prehistoric and meta-historic consciousness, dealing with such realities as Gardens of Eden and Trees of Knowledge of Good and Evil. Our imagination goes only so far in understanding that age, and without relying on symbol and metaphor, most of us would be lost. But directly after the prohibition of tasting the forbidden fruit, we read the first verse of the Bible which has an immediate and relevant bearing on the modern condition: "G-d said, 'It is not good for man to be alone. I will make a help-opposite for him' " (*Bereishis* 2:18). Adam may still be in the Garden of Eden, but who doesn't understand what it means to be alone? With this verse we recognize his flesh and blood reality. His dilemma is our dilemma, and the next paragraph (which should be read

Rabbi Shlomo Riskin is chief rabbi of Efrat, Israel, and dean of the Ohr Torah Institutions.

closely) deals with the major existential issues of humanity, then and now, how the Torah views the fundamental human predicament, the ideal relationship between husband and wife, and the significance of the sexual act between them.

The first problem is the strange Hebrew term, "*eizer kenegdo*," the phrase G-d uses to describe the creature he will provide for Adam in order to conquer his being alone. The literal translation is "a help-opposite." Other translations are "a help-meet" or "a help to match him" or "a compatible helper" — terms which do not fully reflect the inner tension of the concept. Rashi, in explaining the phrase, writes, "if the man is worthy, then his wife will be an *eizer* (a helper); if he is unworthy, she will be *kenegdo* (against him, an opposite force)." Despite Rashi's commentary, a help-opposite is still an unusual term. If it's not good for Adam to be alone, why doesn't G-d simply create a "helper" for him, why an "opposite"?

Second, if G-d is so worried about Adam's being alone, why, in the middle of creating his helper, does the text turn to something different — Adam's naming of the animals? The Torah states, "And the L-rd G-d formed from the earth all of the beasts of the field and all of the fowl of the heavens, and He brought them to man to see what he ought to call them; and whatever man called any of these creatures, that was its name. So man called names to all of the animals and to the fowl of the heavens and to all of the beasts of the field; but man did not find a help-opposite for himself" (*Bereishis* 2:19-20).

This second question is compounded by the fact that the Torah actually seems to be weighing the possibility that Adam's help-opposite might be found among the donkeys, camels, or other four-legged creatures — an amazing idea!

Aloneness has two aspects. First, there is the social loneliness of someone who has no one with whom to share his innermost thoughts and emotions. Several verses back we read that "The Lord G-d formed man of the dust of the ground, and breathed into his nostrils the breath of life, and man became a living soul" (*Bereishis* 2:7). The Targum translates "living soul" as "*ruach memalela* — a spirit that speaks." The act of communication is built into the very psyche of our being. And when a person doesn't have anyone to communicate with, it's tragic.

The second type of aloneness cuts close to the very bone of life and death. We could call it existential aloneness, a concept already alluded to in the Torah because of the infinitive odd form of the verb *heyos* in the verse, *"Lo tov heyos ha'adam levado* — it is not good for man to be alone"* (2:18). In this form, the word *heyos* suggests the existential condition of one's being. "It is not good . . . being . . . man . . . alone" refers to not only being socially alone, but an aloneness which penetrates the depths of one's very existence. Everyone has dreams and aspirations, and whether one realizes most of them, a portion of them, or virtually none of them, the day arrives when one shall embark upon a journey that must be taken alone. The dread of the end, dying, leaving nothing behind, is the mood behind G-d's declaration that "it is not good for man to be alone." No one can join a person for the ride that is the journey of death — not even the people who gave birth to him. Therefore, the Torah is telling us that what a human being desperately needs is a relationship that will help loneliness even in the face of death; apparently, the *eizer kenegdo* can help the human being in respect to both of his needs.

Eizer means help, but the only way the *eizer* can truly help is by having a willingness to limit one's self and allow the other person to stand opposite, not always to agree. A marriage partner is not a geisha-girl to serve drinks and set the table. A life's partner must be able to say no if that is necessary — the *kenegdo* part — because if one marries a yes-sayer, one isn't really being confronted by, or confronting, another. Moreover, the lips may be moving one way, but the heart may be saying no silently, until the heart breaks from the weight of no's. In the end, a "help-opposite" creates its own synthesis, and a new oneness is born. The couple must drink together but not always from the same cup, so that one can correct the other, compliment the other, cheer and comfort the other, help and be helped by the other. Only then is the one not alone.

The second question raised the issue of G-d, Who, understanding Adam's loneliness, suddenly turns to the creatures of the world to be lined up and named by man. This problem is clarified when we realize that when we name something, we define it, and when we define it, we control it — be it a painting we've completed, a pet we've acquired, or a new settlement we're building. However, a relationship of control is not a relationship of complement; it is one-sided and not mutual, taking and not giving. Indeed, humanity is to control the physical, animal world ("And you shall subdue them," is, after all, the divine charge to Adam), but husband is not to control wife. If he does, he has lost out on discovering his *eizer kenegdo*, and overcoming his social loneliness.

And the result of a man-woman relationship of mutuality is the birth of a child, entry into a future beyond their individual life-spans — their gateway to eternity. Since this too is impossible with an "animal" relationship, Adam must be provided with another possibility to assuage his social loneliness and his existential aloneness. Hence, the stage is set for the creation of Chavah, with whom he shall become one flesh, and through whom he, as well as society, can overcome tragic isolation.

Rabbi Hillel Goldberg

Larger than Love

W HAT IS IT?
Love?
In this era and society, marriage not based on love is unusual and, in most cases, unrealistic.

Love? Of course!

But love is love.

Marriage is larger.

Love is personal, and it is for the way one's beloved is now.

Marriage is an institution, and it is for the way one's beloved will unpredictably become.

Love sustains.

But not always.

Love gives life, enthusiasm, character and even inspiration to a marriage.

Love gives a tone, a spark, a beauty.

But not always.

Rabbi Hillel Goldberg, Ph.D., is executive editor of the Intermountain Jewish News, *active in outreach and author of* The Fire Within *(ArtScroll).*

Which is why marriage is larger than love, and *sheva berachos* are about marriage.

About an institution.

About something larger than love.

Something that requires commitment.

Commitment is for difficult times when, especially in this era and this society, many without a Torah perspective suggest, at the first sign of serious difficulty, *end the marriage*.

It's like this. If you are a student in a good school, you might have one poor teacher or one poor class, but you remain *committed* to the school. If your parents are good parents, they may still make mistakes, but you remain *committed* to your parents. Examples are endless. The idea is clear. Marriage is commitment to a person who will inevitably develop in ways not now expected, or will show sides not now known, or will respond to crises in ways not now anticipated.

As an institution, marriage sustains when love cannot stretch that far.

Love is powerful, the most constructively powerful of all human feelings, but sometimes love fluctuates. Marriage is the framework for keeping the embers aflame when, by themselves, they might die out.

This is conveyed by the *sheva berachos*.

". . .*shehakol bara lichvodo*, He created everything for His glory."

What's this? *He*?

His glory?

Do not the *sheva berachos* reflect the most intense, *human* experience?

Not really. The human dimension is given form by an *institution*, by marriage, and this institution is given form by Him.

By G-d.

Love is between two people, while commitment is between two people, as a unit, and G-d.

This is the institution of marriage.

Commitment to G-d.

Something more than love.

And so the *sheva berachos* read: "He created man" and "He created man in His image" and "He gladdens Zion through her children" and "He gladdens groom and bride," and so on. *He*.

G-d.

His institution.

It is more than mutual love and affection and respect, more than any rough spots that might temporarily color that love and affection and respect.

To be committed to the institution of marriage is, like the observance of all other *mitzvos,* to be committed to G-d. Just as those *mitzvos* sustain, build and yield the highest realities precisely because they are constant — one sticks to them throughout every fluctuation of existence — so it is with the *mitzvah* of marriage.

Indeed, this becomes a beautiful thing. People *do* change. Circumstances *do* color the original impetus for love. Hardly least of all, children color the marriage relationship. Precisely so, they are blessings. Precisely the changes and differences that emerge over time become the glories of marriage, *when it is understood to be not only love, but commitment.*

"He creates joy and gladness — *sason vesimcha, chassan vekallah, gilah, rinah, ditzah vechedvah, ahavah ve'achavah veshalom verei'us.*" Again: He. *He* creates all these wonderful things.

Sason and *simcha* are mentioned before *chassan* and *kallah,* since the bride and groom emerge as such only when *sason* and *simcha* take precedence.

When they have independent existence.

When they are rooted in commitment.

In an institution.

In marriage.

Marriage the institution — "*sason vesimcha*" — precedes "*chassan vekallah,*" the individuals.

When that is the case, then the *sason* and *simcha* will last. When the *chassan* and *kallah* understand their union as a frame, a *binyan adei ad,* an *institution* for receiving the blessings that *He* creates, then theirs is the love that will last.

This is the celebration.

Two people committed to each other, and to Hashem *Yisbarach.*

This is marriage.

This is the theme of the *sheva berachos.*

Mandell I. Ganchrow, M.D.

Beriah, Yetzirah, Asiyah

WORDS CAN NOT DESCRIBE the overwhelming emotion one feels having witnessed the union of two people. As sweethearts, your relationship was manifested by an *ahavah rabbah*, a great love, which has now been transformed into a commitment for an *ahavas olam*, an eternal, everlasting love. This moment represents the fruition of your parents' dreams as well. They have seen you grow and mature into dedicated, thoughtful, gracious human beings and *benei Torah*, ready to continue their traditions and way of life. Your union and that of your families affirms that all that your parents have worked for has been successful.

In discussing the first three of the *sheva berachos*, the Maharsha in *Kesubos* describes three terms for creation. The first, *beriah*, is the creation of something from nothing — *ex nihilo*. "In the beginning, G-d created the heavens ..." (*Bereishis* 1:1). This creation, writes the Maharsha, is the spiritual realm represented by the soul. Accordingly, the first *berachah* of *sheva berachos*, "shehakol bara lichvodo," represents the spiritual aspect of man, created in G-d's honor.

The second term is *yetzirah*, as found in the verse, "And the L-rd G-d fashioned (*Vayitzer*) man from the dust of the earth" (*Bereishis* 2:7). This refers to the body, the physical aspects of human beings noted in the second *berachah*, "*yotzeir ha'adam*," and in the third *berachah*, in which we thank the *Ribono Shel Olam*, "*asher yatzar es ha'adam betzalmo*, Who created the human being in His likeness."

The third term is *asiyah*, the creation of a finished product, a human being with a personality, with a Weltanschauung. *Asiyah* is a combination of body and soul, of male and female. The image of G-d and the fusion of personalities reaches into the future to create a *binyan adei ad*, a perpetual structure, adding religious and ethical dimensions to life.

You have both been blessed with great intellect and personality. You are a handsome couple. The *neshamos* given to you at birth have been nurtured by your parents and grandparents, by your brothers and sisters, by your home environments, by your yeshivos and *rabbeim*, by your neighbors and communities. You both understand the great responsibility you undertake as a couple.

You must continue in the tradition handed down not only by those who stand here this evening, but also with those "*asher einenu imanu poh hayom*." They include members of past generations who fled the furnace of Europe, who faced poverty, ill health, trials and tribulations in a new land — and never for a moment gave up their *Yiddishkeit*.

Each of you recognizes that you could excel in your respective careers and still not be a total human being. Your professions represent only the *madah* portion of life. To be a complete Jew, you must perfect your link to Torah and refine your relationships *bein adam laMakom*, *bein adam lachaveiro*, and, as Rav Aaron Soloveitchik has said, *bein adam le'atzmo* — between man and his own conscience. As Jews, we must aim to be truthful to ourselves and to reach our utmost potential. This you have both achieved through your warmth, compassion and dedication to your fellow man. In your professional lives, both of you are symbols of the complete Jew and the complete human being.

My dear *chassan* and *kallah*, your parents and grandparents love you very much. They will always be there to aid and guide you when asked. This *chut hameshulash*, this golden thread of generations of Jewish tradition, charity, communal service, religious commitment and love of Torah, handed down in a chain unbroken, shall never be weakened.

Our prayer and *berachah* to you is that the glow and radiance you project tonight never leave you. May your love for each other flourish. May you fashion your lives so that the *beriah*, your spiritual aspects, and the *yetzirah*, your physical aspects, blend completely through the process of *asiyah* — fusing you into a complete couple that walks *betzelem Elokim*, in the image of G-d. May Hashem give you the *zechus* to build a *binyan adei ad*, the next link in the succession of Torah generations. May Hashem grant you all the wishes and hopes that are in the hearts and prayers tonight of all who love you.

Rabbi Yisroel Saperstein

Communication

THE MOST GLORIOUS POET of the Golden Age of Spain, Ibn Gabirol, proclaimed, "When the roots of love are deeply set in the heart, the branches manifest themselves upon the tongue." How critical it is to remember, when building a marriage, that every word uttered with love and respect builds another bridge between two hearts. Every word spoken sends a message of the deep wells of emotion felt for each other. One should never lose sight of the way words can both draw another close and create a distance.

This idea is hard to integrate into everyday life because kibbitzing and outright putdowns are very stylish in America. Fortunes are spent on "roasts," catered affairs where the guest of honor is made fun of — all in the name of good, clean fun. One must take a step back from this aspect of the American scene in order to build the kind of solid marriage that will withstand the test of time.

Shlomo Hamelech, the wisest of men, wrote, "Death and life are in the power of the tongue" (*Mishlei* 18:21). Nowhere is this proverb truer than in marriage. In order for two people to be able to lower their guard,

---

Rabbi Saperstein is rav of Congregation Kehillas Bais Yehudah in Wesley Hills, New York.

open their hearts, and share with each other their deepest feelings, they must first know they will never be ridiculed or shamed. The beauty and comfort of a wonderful relationship can be destroyed with one careless, degrading remark.

Positive communication is not only about speaking properly; it is also about listening properly — listening with attention, thought and concern to understand the feelings of one's life companion. Not just hearing the words, but hearing how the words are said. For this, too, the Torah provides a model.

When our Matriarch, Sarah, considers her barren state hopeless, she suggests that Avraham take Hagar as a wife that they may have children through her. "*Vayishma Avram lekol Sarai*," the Torah records, "Avram listened to the voice of Sarai" (*Bereishis* 16:2). Why didn't the Torah simply state that "Avram listened to Sarai"? What does the Torah wish to convey by saying that he listened to her voice?

Rav Ovadia Seforno, the Renaissance-era scholar, explains that the Torah is telling the reader that Avraham not only listened to his wife's words but that he paid special to how she spoke them. He paid attention to the tone, to the inflection of her voice. He had to be convinced that she really meant what she said before he would heed her advice.

My dear *chassan* and *kallah,* speaking with consideration and listening with care bring two people so close that they soon understand each other well enough to render words superfluous. As the British parliamentarian and Jewish wit, Lord Mancroft, said, "No man can consider himself truly married until he understands every word his wife is not saying."

Rabbi Moshe S. Gorelik

Goodness

ARRIAGE CREATES A UNIQUE RELATIONSHIP and a special kind of intimacy. The couple begin their journey with hopes and dreams of meaningful experiences together. When the *chuppah* ceremony concludes and the couple walk back up the aisle, hand in hand, amid shouts of *"Mazel tov!"* and the silent prayers of parents and wellwishers, one is inclined to pause for a moment and define the nature of a Jewish marriage and the components that lead to its success.

One finds an inspiring and educational source in the Torah passage that records Hashem's concern for Adam's life in Gan Eden. *"Lo tov heyos ha'adam levado* — It is not good for man to be alone" (*Bereishis* 2:18), says G-d. As the Torah does not record any conversation between Hashem and Adam prior to His creation of Chavah as Adam's mate, a strict reading of the text would indicate that Adam was content with his situation. What was Hashem's motive for declaring Adam's life inadequate? For what reason did Adam require a partner? Was her

---

Rabbi Gorelik is rav of the Young Israel of North Bellmore in North Bellmore, New York.

purpose solely to help him populate the world? If so, she would have been created at the outset, along with him.

The resolution to this question lies in the word *tov*, good. *Tov* has a dual meaning. It includes material benefits and physical pleasures, but also has a moral and spiritual dimension to it. Shlomo Hamelech refers to the Torah as a *"lekach tov"* (*Mishlei* 4:2), a "good doctrine." For a Jew, goodness is defined not only in material terms but also, and more importantly, in spiritual terms. "The good life" requires a moral quality infused into daily living.

Perhaps for this reason, on Rosh Hashanah, Jews wish each other a *"shanah tovah,"* a good year, rather than the secular standard, "Happy new year." A meaningful and successful new year must include spiritual and moral values.

My dear *chassan* and *kallah,* marriage, too, must be enriched by noble ideals. Husband and wife enhance their marriage by sharing a mutual commitment to Torah values. Pragmatic concerns, be they material or emotional, are certainly crucial components contributing to your fulfillment as individuals and as a family. It is imperative, though, to transcend personal needs. You must share in deepening the spirituality of your lives thereby enhancing the moral quality of society.

My dear *chassan* and *kallah,* Hashem declared that Adam could not attain a life of *tov* alone. Only united with Chavah could he do so. Together, as husband and wife, they could infuse their lives with completeness, uniqueness and purpose. May the two of you achieve *tov* together and may Hashem bring you happiness with each other "as G-d made glad His creations in the Garden of Eden."

Rabbi Dr. Moshe D. Tendler

Middah Keneged Middah

R AV HUNA TEACHES THAT ONE who partakes of the *chassan's* meal but does not join in making him happy is considered to have denigrated the blessings of G-d. On the other hand, one who does gladden the *chassan,* states Rav Yehoshua ben Levi, is blessed with Torah knowledge. Rabbi Abahu considers him to have brought a thanksgiving offering. Rav Nachman considers him to have rebuilt one of the destroyed areas of Jerusalem (*Berachos* 6b).

The survival of the Jewish people depends upon the errorless transmission of Torah values from generation to generation. Our Torah leadership, our rabbis, who have been charged with this responsibility, can only teach the truths of Torah. Without the mechanism of the family unit, there is no mode of transmission. It is up to the family unit, and by extension, the community of families, to provide the vehicle for the implementation of these truths. The social conventions and traditions of Torah society can only be perpetuated through the family structure.

For this reason, any behavior that threatens the stability and integrity of the family unit is, according to Torah law, a capital crime. Striking or cursing a parent is punishable by death, as are murder and idolatry; all threaten the ethical and moral lifestyle of the Torah community.

Thus, those who rejoice at a *sheva berachos* meal do not simply share a feast with friends, but rather share in celebrating the establishment of a new family unit and the inauguration of a new vector for the perpetuation of Torah. They are therefore repaid *middah keneged middah*, rewarded in kind with Torah knowledge, says Rav Yehoshua ben Levi.

The celebrants also share in the strengthening of our national mission. Attendance at a *sheva berachos* meal is an expression of personal gratitude and joy at the supportive role this new family will provide in fulfilling the destiny of our great nation. They are, in the words of Rabbi Abahu, considered to have brought a symbolic thanksgiving offering to G-d, "Who chose us from among all the nations and gave us His Torah."

The continued advancement of our nation also brings us one step closer to the final redemption. By sharing in that advancement, as Rav Nachman points out, one contributes to lifting Jerusalem from her ruins.

Chassan and *kallah,* those in attendance are not merely reveling in your joy, but in their own. Your happiness extends to all present because the increased strength of the Jewish community is a national celebration. The pleasure is personal to all gathered here. A new Jewish family furthers our national purpose and brings us one step closer to the final redemption.

Jewish pride swells every chest as families who were exiled centuries ago from their ancestral home lay claim once again to that home. As the Jewish nation continues to rebuild the Holy City, we hear the voice of the prophet, Yirmiyahu (33:11), anticipating "the sound of joy and the sound of happiness, the sound of the groom and the sound of the bride, the sound of those who say, Praise the L-rd of Hosts, for the L-rd is good, for His kindness is everlasting."

Rabbi Menachem Genack

Public vs. Private

THE JEWISH WEDDING CEREMONY provides the quintessential perspective of Jewish life, fusing together seemingly contradictory concepts. The *chuppah* represents the home of the *chassan,* into which he brings his *kallah* to love and to protect. The *chuppah* establishes the most intimate relationship, man and woman bonded together, eyes riveted only on each other, concerned only with each other's needs and desires.

In contrast to this intimacy is the halachic requirement of witnesses to the event as well as the presence of a *minyan* for the reciting of the *sheva berachos*. In fact, the first of those seven blessings, Rashi in *Kesubos* (8a) notes, is made in honor of those present at the event. This gathering serves as a microcosm of the Jewish people.

What is one to make of the paradoxical nature of the *chuppah*? This is the challenge posed to the married Jew, to live simultaneously inside both of these dimensions, one private and one public. A person is responsible, as an individual, to his spouse and family. But he is also responsible to be an active member of the Jewish nation, to further the destiny of his people. Marriage is, therefore, not only a personal celebration, but a communal one, representing another link in the golden chain that connects man to G-d and earth to heaven.

This idea explains another paradoxical ritual. Before entering the *chuppah,* the *chassan* has ashes sprinkled on his head, and under the *chuppah,* he breaks a glass. At the apex of the couple's personal joy, a sense of mourning is introduced in memory of the destroyed Temple in Jerusalem. Their membership in the Jewish people compels them to temper their celebration with reminders that we all continue to live in exile.

Another uniquely Jewish experience: celebration merges with mourning and tears of joy mix with tears of pain.

As they take their place in the Jewish community, the couple commit themselves to the glorious destiny of our people, complete with its peaks and valleys, its rich contrast of lights and shadows that mark the chiaroscuro portrait of our national history.

My dear *chassan* and *kallah,* you are a beautiful example of this dual commitment. Your love for and devotion to each other is intensified by the depth of your commitment to the Jewish faith and the principles of Torah, your concern for fellow Jews, and your love for Eretz Yisrael.

Rabbi Pinchas Stolper

Reuniting Ha-adam

THE SIGNIFICANCE OF THE MARRIAGE BLESSING, *"yotzeir ha'adam*," is often lost in translation, as it is commonly rendered in the past tense — thanking G-d "Who created man." The literal translation of the phrase, however, is in the present tense — thanking G-d "Who is creating man." This is an important distinction. The blessing assumes relevance and immediacy when one realizes that it does not refer to G-d's creation of man at Genesis, an event that happened over five millennia ago, but refers instead to the union taking place before our eyes under the *chuppah*: man and woman joining together to become *ha'adam*.

Who is this joint creature, *ha'adam*? In *Parshas Bereishis*, "G-d created *ha'adam* in His image; in the image of G-d He created him; male and female He created them" (*Bereishis* 1:27). The *pasuk* describes *ha'adam* first in the singular and then in the plural. *Ha'adam* begins as "him" and ends as "them." What is the meaning of this switch?

The first human, explains the Midrash, began as an androgynous being. G-d then divided this being into two halves, two personalities: male and female. This division is described in the *parshah*. "The L-rd G-d put *ha'adam* into a coma and he slept; and He took one of his *tzelaos*" (2:21), from which He formed the first woman. The popular understanding of this *pasuk* is that G-d fashioned Chavah from one of Adam's ribs. But Rashi translates *tzela* more accurately as "side." The first human, which comprised both male and female sides, was then divided into its two component parts.

The goal of marriage is to reunite these two sides, to return them to their original state of *ha'adam*. The Torah's vision of a married couple is higher than the most harmonious, romantic, united-in-eternal-love "we." The Torah's couple creates a new "I," in recognition of G-d's creating man and woman not as separate partners united in a family, but as two complementary halves of a single person, a person designated before birth to transcend its temporary bifurcation and become one again.

Marriage, consequently, is not a simple contractual union; it is the re-fashioning of the "image of G-d" referred to in the verse. Only together, as *ha'adam*, can a couple reflect that which G-d originally intended.

Before splitting *ha'adam*, "The L-rd G-d said, It is not good (*lo tov*) for *ha'adam* to be alone (*levado*)" (2:18). *Levado*, however, signifies more than lonesomeness. It describes a status of individuality, of distinctiveness. The state of *levado* is one of perfection. At the *levado* level, a person has only spiritual desires and inclinations. Nevertheless, the Torah states that it would not be good for *ha'adam* to retain this status of *levado*. Curiously, the Torah does not call this situation bad, *ra*, just not good. What is meant by this description of *lo tov*?

Throughout the description of creation, the Torah repeats the phrase, "G-d saw that it was good (*tov*)," six times. Finally, after man/woman is created, the Torah exclaims, as a finale, "G-d saw everything that he made and it was very good (*tov me'od*)" (1:31). *Tov me'od* is the pinnacle of creation — the ultimate achievement. *Lo tov* is its antithesis. For mankind to be automatically placed in a state of perfection and not have to struggle for it would be *lo tov*. It was not G-d's intention to bestow upon mankind the status of *levado*. G-d wants people to strive to achieve *levado*; He does not want it to be a gift.

If man and woman began their journeys in this world in the perfected state of *levado*, *tov me'od* would not result. To reach perfection, a person must learn to choose good over evil, to elevate and refine his mind, personality and society.

This idea is presented in another *pasuk* that describes G-d as having created everything in this world "to do" (2:31). *Chizkuni* explains that "to do" defines man's obligation in this world: to perfect the world and accomplish those goals the Creator has assigned to him. In that way he will earn his status; he will achieve the level of *levado*.

When a man and woman marry, they acquire the potential to re-capture the state of *levado*, their point of origin, by toiling in Torah and *mitzvos* and perfecting their character through their unique gifts and potential.

Similarly, when Bilam unwittingly blessed the Jews, he described them as "a people living *levadad*, not counted among the nations" (*Bamidbar* 23:9). Bilam saw the Jewish people not as alone, but as independent. They did not need the other nations; they were reliant solely on G-d. This, explains Rashi, is the goal of *levado* in a marriage: to achieve self-sufficiency, to rely on no one but each other. The two partners contribute their maximum efforts and resources, and together their unique contributions create a united independence.

My dear *chassan* and *kallah*, your wedding restores the two of you to the unified state of Adam and Chavah. In marriage, you support and complement each other, reuniting to become a single entity, combining forces to create a home of purpose, sanctity and love.

Mandell I. Ganchrow, M.D.

The Fifth Blessing

I T IS A WELL-KNOWN TENET OF JUDAISM that the highest levels of celebration can not be achieved because of the destruction of our Holy Temple. In the absence of the Temple there is a lack of *complete* happiness even during this, the most important moment in a young couple's life. They are bound by the words of the prophet Yirmiyahu who spoke of what would be after the destruction of the Temple: "I will mute from the cities of Judah and the streets of Jerusalem the sound of joy and the sound of happiness, the sound of the groom and the sound of the bride, for the land shall be laid to waste" (7:34).

It is in memory of the Temple's destruction that the *chassan* has ashes sprinkled on his head and a glass is broken under the *chuppah* while we recite the verse, "If I forget thee, O Jerusalem, let my right hand forget its cunning" (*Tehillim* 137:5).

In the meantime, we bless the couple with *sheva berachos*, the last of which, says the Maharsha (*Kesubos* 8a), was created to emphasize the future completion of the *chassan* and *kallah's* joy when the redemption of the Jewish people comes about and Jerusalem is rebuilt. After the *geulah* their happiness will be fully appreciated and they will celebrate according to the other prophecy of Yirmiyahu: "Again there will be heard. . .in the cities of Judah and the streets of Jerusalem. . .the sound of joy and the sound of happiness, the sound of the groom and the sound of the bride, the sound of those saying, Praise the L-rd" (33:10-11).

In Yirmiyahu's vision of redemption, the Maharsha notes, there is a fifth *kol*, a fifth sound, one that is never muted, never removed from our lips, not even during the period of exile when all the others are suspended. That is the "*kol omrim hodu es Hashem* — the sound of those saying, Praise the L-rd," our thanksgiving prayer to the A-mighty for sustaining us always, even in our darkest days. This fifth *kol* is represented at the end of the fifth *berachah* by "*kol mitzhalos chassanim meichuppasam*, the sound of grooms shouting joyously from their canopies."

As *chassan* and *kallah* prepare to establish their new Jewish home, they give thanks to G-d for their life's good fortune. They pledge that their home will reflect, at least in a small measure, the glory and splendor of the Holy Temple. The Gemara thus teaches that one who rejoices at a wedding is considered to have rebuilt one of the destroyed areas of Jerusalem (*Berachos* 6b).

My dear *chassan* and *kallah*, you have both been blessed, nurtured by the love and kindness emanating from your families. You have been exposed to the finest Torah education, both formal and informal. You have been involved in community projects, in *chessed* programs and in outreach. Your homes have served as models of what a Jewish household should be and you are united in your ambition to replicate such an environment in your own household. In short, you have prepared yourselves for this day.

We share your faith in our covenant and in the vision of Yirmiyahu that predicts the total restoration of Yerushalayim and the building of our Temple. On that day, we will witness a complete return of gladness and joy to you and to all our people. We will see the *kol sason vekol simcha, kol chassan vekol kallah* celebrated to its fullest once again. May your *simcha* tonight be an important step in reaching that goal.

Rabbi Benjamin Blech

Bashert

HERE IS A WORD IN YIDDISH that best captures the meaning of this holy moment. It is a word that summarizes one of the most fundamental principles of our faith, and it has very special significance for you on your wedding day. The word is *bashert* — an amazing concept, which reminds us in the most powerful manner that everything that happens on this earth is part of a Divine master plan, arranged by the A-mighty, with His direction and guidance, for our benefit.

Yes, we do know how you think you met each other. We are well aware of the seeming coincidence of your coming together for the first time. But if you did not already know it then, let us make it clear that your finding each other was in fact a Divine decree preceding even your births.

The Talmud teaches that forty days before one's birth a heavenly voice goes forth and proclaims, "The daughter of so-and-so to so-and-so" (*Sotah* 2a). All that we discovered today was what Hashem

---

Rabbi Blech is rabbi emeritus of the Young Israel of Oceanside in Oceanside, New York.

had intended for each of you a long time ago. And, if you wonder why the heavenly *shidduch* must be arranged so far in advance as to precede even the formation of the child, the answer becomes evident when we look at both of you here together.

G-d decides who belongs together before bodies are formed because He, in His infinite wisdom, decides on the suitability of partners not based on bodies but rather on souls; externals do not concern G-d as much as the compatibility of *neshamos*. It is not because the bride is beautiful or because the groom is handsome that you are deemed worthy to begin a *bayis ne'eman beYisrael* together, but because you share *middos*, values, family traditions, and a commitment to the teachings of the Torah.

You found each other because G-d lit the way before you, to insure that His Divine decree find its fulfillment at this hour. It was *bashert* that you stand here together. For this reason we will be reciting seven blessings — just as G-d created the world in seven days, so too, He is responsible for this union. Seven is the symbol for both the creation of the world as well as the creation of *your* world.

In the context of this remarkable idea one can fully grasp the special choice of two Hebrew words in the concluding blessing recited for you. Our Sages chose the words *sason* as well as *simcha* to describe the elevated feeling of joy at this time. If the Holy Tongue is not content with one term, but requires two different words to express the same notion, then each must possess an individual shade of meaning that distinguishes it from the other.

It was the great Gaon of Vilna who details the difference. Happiness can be caused by two totally different circumstances. When one embarks on a new career, starts an exciting journey, initiates a thrilling new project, he is filled with the joy of potential achievement, the euphoria of yet unrealized possibility, of a glorious still undefined future. Our emotions also know of another kind of happiness. It accompanies the satisfaction of achievement, the gladness of looking back at what has already been accomplished. This is the delight not in what may be, but in what has happened, the gratification of accomplishment.

Hebrew is extremely sensitive to these two types of joy and assigns a different word for each. It is in the Shabbos prayers that we read of the hosts of the heavens, the sun, moon and stars, who delight in their divinely appointed tasks and are *"semeichim betzaisam vesasim bevo'am."* They are filled with the *simcha* of anticipation as they begin their daily rounds and allow themselves the *sason* of satisfaction after they have successfully completed their mandates.

When a child is born we refer to it as a *simcha*, the pleasure of potential. There is no way we can be assured that this newborn will be a source of blessing. But it is a *simcha* because we delight in the opportunity, in what *can* be — that is sufficient. When children reach the age of *bar* and *bas mitzvah,* their celebrations are also called *simchos.* These youngsters are now halachically responsible adults. They face an unknown future. But they and their families feel blessed because these young men and women have the potential to grow into sources of joy and *nachas.*

For these early moments of life we can only use the word *simcha*. At what point can *sason* be introduced? Only at such a time that is life-turning, at the time of marriage, we allow ourselves to hear the *kol sason*, to hear the sound of a different kind of happiness, a joy that emanates from a sense of completion and fulfillment.

My dear *chassan* and *kallah*, you have found each other. You have fulfilled the destiny inscribed upon your souls even before your bodies were formed. You allow your parents, grandparents, relatives and friends to be transported with joy in the realization that what they had prayed for has now come to pass, as you are joined together by Hashem. What makes this moment so special and unique is that at one time there is a *kol sason* and a *kol simcha*. There is the reflection upon your completion of one stage of life; at the same time, there is the blessing defined by the bliss of a new beginning and the potential for a glorious future.

Together you have the possibility to create anew the glories of two magnificent backgrounds. You bring into this marriage the *yichus* of holiness and of greatness. I pray together with everyone here that even as we have been privileged to see so clearly the *sason* of what Hashem has brought together, so may we be able to live to witness and share in the *simcha* of all those accomplishments that lie ahead.

Elliot Ganchrow
(based on a lecture by my rebbe,
Rabbi Mordechai Willig, shlitah.)

Lag Ba'omer

WHY DID THE *GEONIM* choose to commemorate the deaths of Rabbi Akiva's students during the days of *sefirah* over all the other tragedies that befell our nation during its long exile? After all, there have been far greater tragedies in Jewish history with far greater numbers of deaths. Why designate this as a period of national mourning?

Furthermore, why did the *geonim* prohibit weddings during this time? An *aveil*, even during the *sheloshim* period, is allowed to marry. What, therefore, is the connection between marriage and mourning?

Moreover, what is the significance of this period occurring between the holidays of Pesach and Shavuos?

To understand the import of this period, one must first properly understand the Gemara that says that Rabbi Akiva's students did not show respect to one another (*Yevamos* 62b). The Gemara does not mean that when the students came into the *beis medrash* each morning they did not say to each other, "Hello, how are you?" or that they were not polite to each other. These were *talmidei chachamim* — of course they were polite.

Elliot Ganchrow is a junior at Yeshiva University.

Thus when the Gemara says they showed no respect, it must mean a special kind of respect, a higher standard of honor that one *chaveir* must show to the other. When one is studying Torah he must show a level of respect loftier than that which he would show a friend on the street. Especially at Rabbi Akiva's time, a time when all Torah was still studied orally, when the Gemara had yet to be written, a higher degree of respect was mandatory. This special treatment is what was missing among his students.

The Gemara alludes to the cause of their death with its statement that 12,000 *pairs* of students perished, for it was their improper behavior toward each other as pairs — *chavrusos* studying Torah together — that led to their demise. Theirs was not a standard, friendly relationship, but a relationship of Torah.

This is why their loss must be commemorated more than other losses. Torah is our backbone; it is our essence. If we do not know how to learn Torah properly, if we do not understand that a Torah discussion is no ordinary streetside conversation, then we are lost.

For this reason, the period leading up to Shavuos, during which we prepare ourselves to receive the Torah, is the ideal time to remind ourselves of this all-important principle. If we do not know how to learn Torah, if we are not prepared to sit down with our *chavrusos* and learn as proper *benei Torah*, then *mattan Torah* is for naught.

For this very reason also, weddings are prohibited during this time. Marriage is the choosing of a lifelong *chavrusah*, a partner with whom to build a family of Torah. The higher level of honor that one must give a learning partner is the same that one must give a marriage partner. The degree of respect that one shows to a spouse must surpass that which one shows to a regular friend. If this respect is lacking, then the marriage is not based on the principles of Torah and the relationship is headed for disaster.

My dear *chassan* and *kallah,* all of us who celebrate these moments with you pray that you share a life of harmony and understanding, embracing the principles of Torah so that you act in concert with one another to achieve *shalom* and love.

Rabbi J. Simcha Cohen

Marriage Tones

A WEDDING IS A VERY PERSONAL, private experience. Yet, tradition insists that the most deep-seated emotions of marriage must be vocalized. It is not sufficient that the innermost sensitive chords of a bride and bridegroom strum with a melody of joy; there must also be the actual sounds or tones of happiness. This is evident in the *berachah* to the bride and bridegroom wherein it is stated, "*kol sason vekol simcha, kol chassan vekol kallah.*" Each emotion mandates a sound.

First there is the *kol sason*. This relates to the happiness of receiving unanticipated good fortune. It is based on the verse, "*Sas anochi* — I am happy with Your word [Torah] as one who finds great spoil" (*Tehillim* 119:62). The Vilna Gaon notes that one does not begin a day seeking a lost treasure. Yet, should he find one, his joy is immense. The bride and bridegroom are blessed with the wish that unprogrammed good tidings enhance their lives.

A married couple should also have *kol simcha*. This relates to the excitement of newness, to a sensation of perceiving or acquiring something for the first time. It is a feeling tinged with a sense of wonder and amazement. This is the meaning of the *berachah* to the bride and bridegroom in which the new couple is blessed with the *simcha* of Adam and Chavah in the Garden of Eden. In the Garden of Eden, all life was an adventure. Everything was new, fresh and unique.

Simcha also refers to the joy of accomplishment, It is the happiness crystallized through the attainment of the fruits of labor. For this reason Sukkos is termed *zeman simchaseinu*, the season of our happiness. At harvest time, there is an exhilarating sense of satisfaction in seeing that efforts have come to fruition.

There is also a special sound of a bride and bridegroom, a *"kol chassan vekol kallah."* These sounds relate to the softness, the gentility, the loving manner, in which a bride and bridegroom address each other. These feelings must be articulated. These concerns must be heard. Not only during marriage but also throughout the never-ending tomorrows of the future.

No Jew may marry without witnesses present. *Klal Yisrael* must witness the event. Happiness is not to be a private emotion, but one shared with one's people. The tradition of the tones of happiness — *kol sason vekol simcha* — generates the concept that *Klal Yisrael* must also witness these audible expressions of joy. The prayer of all present is that the bride and bridegroom forever cherish these tones of happiness.

Rabbi Yitzchok Adlerstein

A Marriage Trilogy:
The Hidden Power
of the Jewish Marriage
According to Maharal

R AV YEHUDAH LOEW OF PRAGUE, usually referred to as Maharal, ranks among the most important interpreters of the *aggadic* tradition. His thoughts on obscure passages of the Midrash make them come alive with rich symbolism and mystical allusion.

Maharal was one of very few rabbinic authors to write independent works in addition to publishing commentary to earlier texts. In chapter 30 of one such work, *Tiferes Yisrael*, his study on the nature of Torah, Maharal considers the significance of the furious sounds that accompanied the giving of the Torah at Mount Sinai (*Shemos* 19:15). Having offered his explanation of this clamor, he then turns to a Talmudic passage (*Berachos* 6b) that compares these sounds to those that celebrate a Jewish wedding. His analysis offers some fascinating perspectives on the inner meaning of a Jewish wedding and motivates the reader to celebrate its *simcha* more fully.

Rabbi Adlerstein is director of the Jewish Studies Institute of the Yeshiva of Los Angeles in Los Angeles, California.

Rabbi Chelbo said in the name of Rav Huna, "Whoever enjoys the wedding meal without gladdening the groom violates five 'sounds,' as it is written, '. . .the sound of rejoicing and the sound of happiness, the sound of the groom and the sound of the bride, the sound of those who say, Praise the L-rd' (Yirmiyahu 33:11). "And if he does bring happiness to the groom what is his reward? Rabbi Yehoshua ben Levi said, "He merits the Torah, which was given with five sounds . . .." Rabbi Abahu said, "He is considered to have brought a thanksgiving offering . . .." Rabbi Nachman said, "He is considered to have rebuilt one of the destroyed areas of Jerusalem."

These three opinions offer different insights into the importance of marriage and can be appreciated only after one reflects on the symbolism that each employs.

Marriage as Personal Arrival

Rabbi Chelbo focuses on the notion of sound. Noise is the inevitable by-product of activity. Someone who has accomplished something tells his friends with fanfare and a flourish, not quietly. Sound connotes existence itself. Things that move whir and buzz and hum, telling us that something is happening.

As something approaches perfection, more of its parts and capabilities are actualized, more of it comes into its own, into existence, and as that happens, it makes itself heard. Nothing can be lulled into silence unless part of it has been suppressed.

One can thus readily understand why the giving of the Torah was accompanied by multiple sounds. The Torah is the plan for the world, an order imposed by the absolute perfection of G-d, but as long as it was not available to man, the Torah remained unfulfilled, stifled. Becoming a part of this world was an expression of its power to set things right. The sheer intellectual power of the Torah shifted from potential to actual on that sixth day of Sivan, and as it did, as it came more fully into being, it made itself heard with multiple sounds.

Five sounds, to be exact, our Sages count. Four of these sounds represent the four directions to which the Torah broke out from a fifth, central point of origin, projecting itself in every possible direction. When the Torah arrived, it created more than a single sonic boom; it reached into every nook and cranny of creation, spreading out forever and beyond. Its perfection knows no containment.

This model sustains Rabbi Yehoshua ben Levi's view of marriage. People sing and dance at a wedding not just because they share the joy of two people who love and cherish each other, but because they are witness to Creation. Man, the most perfect of all the creatures G-d placed on earth, is not complete without a spouse. Man does not simply become happier with marriage. He *becomes.* Two human beings are actualized and perfected by joining with each other.

Every individual has the power to project, influence and extend to the far reaches of the cosmos, just as the Torah does. But man can only do this in his perfected state, a state he enters only with marriage. When friends and family celebrate this being created in the image of his Master, they cannot fail to hear the explosion of a newly unleashed power. One can only remain unmoved if he is insensitive to the mission and purpose of a Jewish life, for when one understand the magnificent beauty with which G-d has endowed each Jew, one cannot fail to celebrate alongside the *chassan* and *kallah.*

Divine Glue

> *Rabbi Abahu said, He is considered to have brought a thanks-giving offering.*

Strange thing, the *korban todah*, the thanksgiving offering. The Torah ordinarily objects to the inclusion of *chameitz* in any offering brought in the Temple. But for the *todah*, the Torah demands it.

Some things do not mix well. The last thing you want to find on a piece of matzah during Pesach is a hot slice of french toast. (But a week after Pesach, you had better serve your guests the cream cheese and lox on a fresh bagel, not another piece of *shemurah* matzah.) *Chameitz* and matzah are just not agreeable soulmates, and, seen as symbols, it becomes easy to understand why.

Rabbinic literature is peppered with references to *chameitz* as symbolic of the *yeitzer hara*, man's evil inclination. Leave a chunk of dough idle for awhile and invisible yeast cells will float in, uninvited, helping themselves to a scrumptuous repast of sugar molecules. They begin their chemical mischief and release carbon dioxide, which sours the dough.

Judaism views evil as working much the same way. All it takes for good people to succumb to it is to remain idle. Do nothing and the inner voice that urges evil behavior enters and never seems to leave, souring the prospects for good.

Matzah, on the other hand, represents the opposite, the *yeitzer hatov*, man's inclination toward the good and proper. Mixing the *chameitz* with the matzah, the evil with the good, would create a poorly mixed metaphor, a confusing combination of contradictory elements. Certainly the Holy Temple is no place to introduce these two diametrically opposed ingredients.

But the *todah* calls for just that. It is the exception.

Who brings a *korban todah*? Someone who has had a close encounter with life-threatening peril. Having confronted his naked mortality and having emerged intact, he feels small and vulnerable, recognizing that the hand of G-d has touched him. The obscurity of everyday life is lifted by this clarity. He suddenly understands, as never before, that his life and all the forces that threaten it belong completely to Hashem, that everything in existence owes itself to G-d. Even polar opposites. Even good and evil, matzah and *chameitz*.

Thus, "In the [Messianic] future, all offerings will be nulified, but the thanksgiving offering will not be nullified" (*Vayikra Rabbah* 9:7). What is the connection? Because at the end of days "G-d will become One and His Name One" (*Zechariah* 14:9). People will recognize that all the disparate, competing forces that surround them are united by the will of G-d. Beyond the differences and tensions lies the absolute unity of G-d Himself. The *todah*, with its blend of the seemingly incompatible, serves as the perfect offering for the Messianic age.

Marriage enjoys some of this incompatibility. Moving beyond romantic notions of perfect matches, there remains a dimension of difference that separates two individuals. There are gaps-chasms, really-that divide the identities of all people. Bringing these differences together, especially those of men and women, is a formidable task. Those who stood before the *chuppah* were conscious of how dependent we are on Hashem to bring opposites together and to cement them into a new couple despite the barriers.

When dancing before the new couple, one attempts to increase their joy and their affection for each other, bringing them closer yet. In celebrating their marriage, one occupies himself in G-d's work, nudging together two pieces of an inherently imperfect fit. Without an altar, one still succeeds in bringing a *korban todah*.

Heavenly Synthesis

Rav Nachman said, He is considered to have rebuilt one of the destroyed areas of Jerusalem.

Three international faiths revere the city of Yerushalayim. They have killed and been killed for her and still call her their own. But only Jews understand her inner meaning, only they comprehend that she is not just a city of history, a place touched by the confluence of great events and great people, but literally *Ir Shaleim* — The City of Perfection.

A city is the dwelling place of many. In a perfected state, she can be the catalyst for a collective effort that spills over her boundaries. Yerushalayim in her years of glory was such a place. Housing the *Shechinah* in her midst, her citizens were able hosts to Divinity, and their nobility, their pure spirituality, became a beacon to the entire world.

But it did not last. Yerushalayim's citizens did not remain up to the task of being human counterparts to the angelic residents of her spiritual sister city, *Yerushalayim Shel Maalah*, the Jerusalem Above. Stripped of her spiritual promise, her physical presence followed suit. The city was destroyed, her buildings left to ruin.

They await rebuilding, for the day when Moshiach will arrive and claim Yerushalayim as his capital, the place from which he will launch an international campaign of uniting the world under the Kingdom of G-d.

In the meantime, the Jewish community continues to work toward that goal. Every step we take in the direction of universal good helps to restore Yerushalayim's ruins. With every marriage celebrated among our people, the finishing touches are placed on another edifice, says Rav Nachman. The final dimension of marriage that should be considered is that *chassan* and *kallah* help advance Hashem's plan for the unfolding of history. What they create between them is a vehicle to marry His will to life in this world. The combination of forces that shape the Jewish household also provide a dramatic step toward *tikun olam*.

My dear *chassan* and *kallah*, your marriage is not only a *simcha* of *chassan* and *kallah*, it is a *simcha* of Hashem Himself. And as we rejoice with you, we rejoice with Him.